Quality Assessment in High Schools

Accounts From Teachers

Quality Assessment in High Schools

Accounts From Teachers

Anne Davies, Ph.D.
Sandra Herbst
Kathy Busick, Ph.D.

A Joint Publication

Solution Tree

Connections Publishing

Published in the US by Solution Tree Press
555 North Morton Street
Bloomington, IN 47404
800.733.6786 (toll free) / 812.336.7700
FAX: 812.336.7790
email: info@solution-tree.com
solution-tree.com

Printed in the United States of America.

17 16 15 14 13   1 2 3 4 5

Library of Congress Cataloging-in-Publication Data

Davies, Anne, 1955-
  Quality assessment in high schools : accounts from teachers / Anne Davies, Ph. D., Sandra Herbst, Kathy Busick, Ph. D.
     pages cm
  Includes bibliographical references and index.
  ISBN 978-1-935543-97-8 (perfect bound) 1. Educational tests and measurements. 2. Education, Secondary.
I. Herbst, Sandra, 1970- II. Busick, Kathleen U. III. Title.
  LB3051.D3656 2013
  371.26--dc23
                                        2013004961

Solution Tree
Jeffrey C. Jones, CEO
Edmund M. Ackerman, President

Solution Tree Press
President: Douglas M. Rife
Publisher: Robert D. Clouse
Editorial Director: Lesley Bolton
Managing Production Editor: Caroline Wise

Connections Publishing
Cover Art and Book Design: START Communications
Cover Photo: www.free-pictures-photos.com
Editing: Annie Jack
Project Management: Judith Hall-Patch

Contents

Foreword

Travel back to school in your mind's time machine. Your English teacher has just handed back your paper full of red corrections and a big red *D*, expressing frustration at your lack of achievement and threatening an *F* on your report card if you don't get going. Or you're in middle school science class and your teacher startles everyone by instructing, "Take out a blank sheet of paper for a pop quiz." Or you are in speech class and learn that your final speech will count for half of your grade. Or your guidance counselor spells out in specific detail the dire consequences of college admissions test scores.

What do these scenarios have in common? They all reflect the belief among at least some of the teachers of our youth that the way to maximize motivation and, therefore, learning is to maximize the anxiety of the learner, and the intimidation of assessment is the way to do it. The more on edge students were, these teachers believed, the harder they would study and the more they would learn. To get more learning, demand it more vigorously; invoke the negative consequences of failure; use adult authority to hold students accountable for more learning; if a little intimidation doesn't work, turn up the heat with a lot of intimidation. These were familiar emotional dynamics of assessment for most of us during our schooling years. Essentially, the role of assessment was to perpetuate a constant state of fear. The key to effective schools was to scare students into learning.

Assessment as a Matter of Emotional Dynamics

This belief about the role of assessment merged neatly into the mission of the schools of our youth, which was to rank us from the highest to the lowest achiever by the end of high school. One function of schools was to begin to sort us into the various segments of our social and economic system. The amount of time available to learn was fixed: one year per grade. The amount learned by the end of that time was free to vary: some of us learned a great deal, some very little. Able learners built on past successes to grow rapidly. However, students who failed to master the early prerequisites within the allotted time failed to learn that which followed. After thirteen years of cumulative treatment in this manner, in effect, we were spread along an achievement continuum that literally labeled each student's rank in class upon graduation.

The emotional dynamics of this process were clear. From the very earliest grades, some students rode winning streaks. Right from the start, they scored high on assessments. The emotional effect of this was to help them come to believe themselves to be capable learners—they became increasingly confident in school. That gave them the emotional strength to risk striving for more success because, in their minds, success was within reach if they tried. Notice, by the way, that the trigger for their learning success was *their interpretation of their own success* on assessments.

But other students scored very low on tests right from the beginning. This caused them to doubt their own capabilities as learners. They began to lose confidence, which, in turn, deprived them of the emotional reserves to continue to risk trying. Chronic failure was hard to hide and became embarrassing. Better not to try. As their motivation waned, of course, achievement followed. Notice again how the learners' own interpretation of assessment results influenced their confidence and willingness to strive on.

In the schools of our youth, if some students worked hard and learned a lot, that was a positive result, as they would finish high in the rank order. And if some students gave up in hopeless failure, that was a necessary result too, because they would occupy places very low in the rank order. The greater the spread of achievement from top to bottom, the more dependable would be the rank order. This is why, if a student gave up and stopped trying (even dropped out of school), it was regarded as that student's problem, not the teacher's or school's. The school's responsibility was to provide the opportunity to learn. If students didn't take advantage of the opportunity, that was not the system's responsibility.

Some students respond to tougher academic challenges by working hard and learning, while others are driven to minimize their accumulating anxiety by escaping from the source—that is, by giving up in hopelessness. The result for the latter group? Exactly the opposite of the one society wants—they learn much less, not more. So, in effect, these intimidation-driven assessment practices have the effect of driving down the achievement of as many students as they have elevated; they have promoted as many losing streaks as winning streaks.

The important lesson we must learn is that students' emotional reactions to assessment results will determine what they think, feel, and do in response to those results. They can respond one of two ways to any classroom or large-scale assessment, one productive and the other not. The productive reaction has students seeing the results and saying, "I understand these results. I know what to do next to learn more. I can handle this. I choose to keep trying." The counterproductive response leaves students saying, "I don't know what these results mean for me. I have no idea what to do next. I can't handle this. I quit."

If society wants all students to meet standards, then, as a precondition, all students must believe they can meet those standards; they all must be confident enough to be willing to take the risk of trying. Any other emotional state (such as the state of perpetual fear perpetrated in the schools of our youth) for any student is unacceptable. We can't have students who have yet to meet standards losing faith in themselves and giving up in hopelessness.

As a society, over the past decade, we have come to understand that our ongoing and accelerating technical evolution and increasing ethnic diversity will demand citizens who are lifelong learners. We also have come to see that, in the above environment, students in the bottom third of the rank order, plus all who drop out without being ranked, fail to develop the foundational reading, writing, and math problem-solving proficiencies needed to function effectively in the future. As a result, society has asked its educators to raise the bottom of the rank order distribution to a certain level of achievement. We call these expectations our academic achievement standards. Every state and province has them and, as a matter of public policy, schools are to be held accountable for making sure all students meet those standards.

Now, as a result, assessment practices that permitted, even encouraged, some students to give up on learning must be replaced by those that engender hope and sustained effort for all. In short, the entire emotional environment surrounding the experience of being evaluated must change, especially for perennial low achievers.

The driving emotional force of fear triggered by the prospect of an upcoming test must be replaced by confidence, optimism, and persistence—for all students, not just for some. All students must believe that, *I can succeed at learning if I try.* They must have continuous access to credible evidence of their own academic success. This has spawned intense interest in assessment *for* learning—assessment used day to day by students and their teachers working together to maintain student confidence and to sustain learning success.

Assessments Must Inform the Learner Too

This emotional dimension of the student's assessment experience interacts directly with an associated intellectual dimension that is every bit as important as the emotional. The intellectual facet centers on the instructional decisions students make about their learning, based on their own interpretation of assessment results.

Over the decades, both school improvement experts and the measurement community have made the mistake of believing that the adults in the system are the most important assessment users/instructional decision makers; that is, we have believed that, as the adults make better instructional decisions, schools will become more effective. Clearly, parents, teachers, school leaders, and policy makers make crucial decisions that influence the quality of schools, and the more data based those decisions are, the better. But this discounts the fact that students may be even more important data-based instructional decision makers than the adults.

Consider, for example, the reality that students are constantly deciding if they can do the learning. They ask, "Can I get this stuff, or am I just too dense? Is the learning worth the energy I must expend to attain it? Is the learning worth the risk of public failure?" We must understand that, if students come down on the wrong side of these crucial decisions and, thus, stop trying, it doesn't matter what the adults around them decide. In effect, our students can render our instructional decisions null and void. They have it in their power to make us ineffective and to prevent us from doing anything about it. I don't mean that they would do so intentionally. But if a student decides that the learning is beyond reach for her or him or that the risk of public failure is too great and too humiliating, then regardless of what we adults do, there will be no learning.

So the essential issue for us adults is: *What can we do to help students answer the above questions in ways that keep them trying?* We know how to do that, and it is not by intensifying the intimidation! Furthermore, we know what will happen to student achievement when we put effective classroom assessment practices in place. Let me explain specifically what that means.

A Productive Dynamic: Classroom Assessment *for* Student Learning

Assessment *for* learning turns the classroom assessment process and its results into an instructional intervention designed to increase, not merely monitor, student learning. Research evidence gathered in hundreds of studies conducted, literally, around the world over the past decade, shows that the consistent application of principles of assessment *for* learning can give rise to unprecedented gains in student achievement, especially for perennial low achievers. The implications for such gains in raising test scores and closing achievement score gaps are profound.

To understand how these practices impact student learning, one must begin with a general sense of how assessment fits into instruction. We assess to draw inferences about student achievement for two reasons: to inform instructional decisions and to encourage students to try.

If assessment is, at least in part, the process of gathering evidence to inform instructional decisions, then the key starting questions for any assessment are: What decisions? Who's making them? and What information will be helpful? In the case of assessment *for* learning, the key question is: *What comes next in the learning?* The key classroom decision makers are teachers *and their students.* And the information required centers on *where the student is now* in the progression of learning leading up to mastery of each academic achievement standard. The idea is never to leave students wondering where they are now, what success looks like, and how to close the gap between the two. Students must never question *whether* they will succeed. Incremental success is always within reach.

Key Features and Roles

Perhaps the most unique feature of the assessment *for* learning process is that it acknowledges the critical importance of the instructional decisions made by students and their teachers, working as a team—it provides the information they need when they need it. In that context, students become consumers of assessment information too, using evidence of their own progress to understand what comes next for them.

Another unique feature is its reliance on standards-based curriculum maps, written in easily understandable versions for teachers, students, and family members, so that the trajectory (i.e., what has been learned and what comes next) is clear to all throughout the learning. This leads directly to our second reason for assessing: if we assess to motivate students to try, assessment *for* learning enables students by helping them watch themselves grow—by causing them to believe that success is within reach if they keep trying.

Thus, it becomes clear that assessment *for* learning cannot happen just once a year or quarterly or even weekly. It must continue throughout the learning. To accomplish this, the teacher's classroom assessment role must play out in five parts:

1. Become competent masters themselves of each of the standards their students are to master.

2.   Understand how those standards transform into the curriculum that forms the scaffolding students will climb on their journey up to each standard.

3.   Make those classroom-level achievement targets clear to students.

4.   Transform the classroom targets into high-quality classroom assessments, capable of accurately reflecting student achievement of those targets.

5.   Use those assessments over time in collaboration with their students to inform key decisions and to help motivate students to keep learning.

One strategy teachers rely on in assessment *for* learning classrooms is to provide students with a *clear vision* of the learning target from the beginning of the learning, along with *samples* of strong and weak work so they can see a progression to competence laid out before them. This builds confidence among learners by revealing the path to success. Another is to provide students with regular access to *descriptive* (versus evaluative or judgmental) feedback; that is, information that helps students understand how to improve the quality of their work. This requires repeated *self-assessments* so they can watch themselves successfully negotiating the road to competence. As students watch themselves succeeding, again, they become increasingly confident. Ultimately, students can learn to generate their own *descriptive feedback* (that is, learn to self-assess) and to *set goals* for what comes next in their learning. Each of these specific practices draws the learner more deeply into monitoring and taking responsibility for her or his own success.

Thus, the student's role in assessment *for* learning environments is to strive to understand what success looks like and to use each assessment to determine how to do better the next time. Assessments become more than one-time events attached to the end of the teaching. They become part of the learning process by keeping students posted on their progress and confident enough to continue striving.

From Formative Assessment to Assessment *for* Learning

Assessment *for* learning is different from what historically has been referred to as "formative assessment." If formative assessment is about gathering evidence more frequently, assessment *for* learning is about gathering it continuously. If formative assessment is about teachers gathering and using evidence of learning, assessment *for* learning is about students gathering and using information about themselves, too. If formative assessment tells users who is and is not meeting state standards, assessment *for* learning tells them what progress each student is making toward mastering each standard *while the learning is happening*—when there's still time to be helpful.

Assessment *for* learning is obviously different from summative assessment, which asks, Which students have reached the top of the scaffolding? These tests hold students and their teachers accountable for meeting required standards, as they should. They judge the sufficiency of learning at a particular point in time. State and district assessments, as well as classroom assessments for report card grading, represent examples of summative assessment.

In the perfect assessment system, one would seek to balance these various assessment purposes. The foundation would be a continuous array of assessments *for* learning used to help students learn more—to lead them along through increments of success. In addition, periodic early warning benchmark assessments would help teachers see student progress in terms of standards mastered, revealing to them who needs help with greater frequency than has been provided by once-a-year assessments. And finally, once-a-year accountability tests would rely on a variety of appropriate assessment formats (not merely multiple-choice tests) to verify the ultimate level of student success. This balanced pattern promises to meet the information needs of all assessment users.

Research on Effects

When assessment *for* learning practices play out as a matter of routine in classrooms, as mentioned previously, evidence gathered around the world consistently reveals effect sizes of a half to one and a half standard deviations and more, directly attributable to the application of classroom assessment *for* learning. In his original mastery learning research, Bloom and his students (1984) make extensive use of classroom assessment in support of learning, in just the same terms as does the assessment *for* learning concept being described here, and report subsequent gains in student test performance of one to two standard deviations. Black and Wiliam, in their 1998 watershed research review of more than 250 studies from around the world on the impact of effective classroom assessment, report gains of a half to a full standard deviation, with the largest gains being realized by low achievers. According to these researchers, the expected achievement score gains will rival in their impact on student achievement the implementation of one-on-one tutorial instruction, with the largest gains being realized by the lowest achievers, thus reducing achievement gaps.

But We Are Unprepared to Assess *for* Learning

But the severe and chronic problem is that very few teachers and almost no school administrators have been given the opportunity to learn about principles of sound assessment practice of any sort, let alone assessment *for* learning. While virtually all licensing standards require competence in assessment, typically neither preservice nor in-service teacher or administrator training programs include this kind of training (Crooks, 1988; Stiggins, 1999; Shepard et al., 2005). As a result of this lack of preparation:

1. Educators are unable to differentiate among the various information needs of different assessment users, including students.

2. Achievement targets remain written at the state or district standards level rather than being translated into classroom-level learning progressions that lead up to each standard.

3. The risk of inaccurate classroom assessments remains high.

4. Feedback provided to students remains evaluative (such as grades) versus helpfully descriptive.

5. Students are rarely involved in self-assessment, tracking their own progress, or communicating their learning to others, all of which can give rise to profound learning gains.

The current state of affairs is clear: we know what teachers and administrators need to know and understand to assess effectively day to day in the classroom (Stiggins, Arter, Chappuis, and Chappuis, 2004). It is clear what will happen to student confidence, motivation, and learning if they do so. And we know how to deliver the proper classroom assessment competence into their hands with efficient and effective professional development (Stiggins and Chappuis, 2006). The only unanswered question is, *Will practitioners be given the opportunity to learn to assess* for *learning?* Historically, the answer has been an unequivocal no. As a result, the immense potential of assessment *for* learning has gone untapped. It need not be so.

Rick Stiggins
Assessment Training Institute
Portland, Oregon

References

Black, P., and Wiliam, D. (1998). Assessment and classroom learning. *Educational Assessment: Principles, Policy & Practice, 5*(1), 7–74. Also summarized in an article titled Inside the black box: Raising standards through classroom assessment. *Phi Delta Kappan, 80*(2), 139–148.

Bloom, B. (1984). The search for methods of group instruction as effective as one-to-one tutoring. *Educational Leadership, 41*(8), 4–17.

Crooks, T. J. (1988). The impact of classroom evaluation on students. *Review of Educational Research, 58*(4), 438–481.

Shepard, L., Hammerness, K., Darling-Hammond, L., Rust, F., Snowden, J. B., Gordon, E., Gutierrez, C., and Pacheco, J. (2005). Assessment. In L. Darling-Hammond & J. Bransford (Eds.). *Preparing teachers for a changing world: What teachers should know and be able to do* (pp. 275–326). San Francisco: Jossey-Bass. (Note particularly pp. 282–284.)

Stiggins, R. J. (1999). Evaluating classroom assessment training in teacher education. *Educational Measurement: Issues and Practice, 18*(1), 23–27.

Stiggins, R. J., Arter, J., Chappuis, J., and Chappuis, S. (2004). *Classroom assessment for student learning: Doing it right—Using it well.* Portland, OR: Assessment Training Institute.

Stiggins, R. J., and Chappuis, J. (2006). What a difference a word makes: Assessment *for* learning rather than assessment *of* learning helps students succeed. *Journal of Staff Development, 27*(1), 10–14.

Prologue

The Belted Kingfisher is a common waterside resident in British Columbia. It is often seen hovering above, peeping down and examining its target before plunging headfirst into the water. The Kingfisher Series is sponsored by the group of educators who have gathered annually since 2000 for a week of intense learning and reflection, using classroom assessment practices. These lead learners come together to rise above and reflect on their work, to survey the challenges they face in their daily practice, and to focus on their goal of more effectively supporting learners. Then they leave to plunge, once again, into their chosen work. This book invites you to peer through the eyes of high school educators and take the plunge into quality assessment.

Meeting the challenges that arise from the classroom assessment research findings—particularly assessment in the service of learning—is not an easy task. High schools are decidedly demanding environments without the additional challenge of learning and developing a new teaching practice. However, the educators who have contributed to this text are convinced that the effort is well worthwhile. Their examples and accounts demonstrate how assessment can actually make the educator's job easier and more effective for both students and teachers.

Our intention is to inform and support high school teachers and those who support high school teachers in their work, as they engage in learning about what is working and what might need to change so that classroom assessment practices directly support student learning. The authors of these chapters come from a variety of disciplines—English, world languages, social studies, mathematics, science, creative writing, philosophy, alternative education, fine arts, journalism and media—because we know that while some assessment practices are similar across disciplines, there are also variations of practices that are unique to different disciplines.

Each author writes from his or her personal experience and perspective—sharing struggles, concrete examples, and hard-won insights. Some have many years of experience, and others are in the early stages of their professional lives. Each has risked inviting students into the assessment process without a "net." Each models with students and colleagues what it means to learn from missteps, to seek feedback, to keep a sense of humor, and to apply insights from both failures and successes in order to strengthen their students' learning. Their individual and combined voices affirm the power of quality classroom assessment and bring it into reality in their practice. Together, their voices affirm the power of classroom assessment to increase learning across different disciplines and school systems. They provide a rainbow of strategies and pathways for teaching and learning success. As they offer an array of possibilities, they invite readers to join in and make a difference for learning in their own settings. This book is divided into three sections:

- Preparing for learning, teaching, and assessment

- Activating and engaging learners using assessment

- Preparing to evaluate and report

As you read, reflect on your own assessment practices. We invite you to identify ideas or refinements that might support you and your students.

Section One
Preparing for Learning, Teaching, and Assessment

Section One:
Preparing for Learning, Teaching, and Assessment

As teachers prepare to engage with students and use quality classroom assessment, they make plans. They seek worthwhile learning activities that will not only help the students learn but also generate rich collections of evidence or proof of learning. This preparation for student learning begins with getting ready for quality classroom assessment. As you read the chapters in this section, notice that these teachers:

1. Prepare to communicate the standards or outcomes that need to be taught (and learned by students)
2. Understand the expected quality and achievement levels for the given grade level, content area, or course expectations
3. Have identified potential evidence of learning that will result from activities, tasks, projects, and other learning opportunities
4. Are collecting and recording reliable and valid evidence of learning

1 In the first chapter, **Brent McKeown** and **Scott Horton**, teachers of English and student leadership in Edmonton, Alberta, discuss the challenge of creating a meaningful classroom assessment system in the midst of system requirements, such as final examinations marked centrally and worth 50 percent of a student's final grade. Success, in terms of student engagement and ownership, is signaled by students who ask questions such as, "What do I need to do to be able to demonstrate that I can achieve this course outcome?"

2 **Holly Clark Tornrose**, an English teacher in Yarmouth, Maine, discusses the power of a clear purpose in successfully balancing classroom, school, and district needs for evidence of learning. She explains how she prepares for each and assesses her courses. Then she demonstrates how she involves students deeply in the process of collecting evidence of learning in relation to course standards.

3 **Philip Divinsky**, a vocational teacher, and **Thomas Lafavore**, director of Educational Planning for Portland (Maine) Public Schools, write about involving students with special needs in developing a community of learners in an alternative high school program. By building classroom agreements, teacher and students create a safe and collaborative environment in which learners can take risks, receive productive feedback, and believe themselves capable of learning and producing quality work.

4 **Alice Yates** illustrates how she plans and then uses classroom assessment practices in a modern language course to involve students and help them learn. She documents her successes with a multilevel class in her Maine high school.

5 In the last chapter in this section, **Sandra Herbst** writes about Rob Hadath's grade 12 mathematics class. It is just three days before the end of the term and the provincial exam and yet Rob Hadath is still using assessment in the service of learning.

Brent McKeown, B.A., B.Ed., M.Ed., is assistant principal at T. D. Baker School in Edmonton, Alberta.

Brent McKeown & Scott Horton

Brent and Scott undertook the work described in this chapter while they were colleagues in the English department at M. E. Lazerte High School. They continue their collaborative efforts in teaching, assessment, and writing and have devoted much of their recent energies to sharing their ideas, techniques, and experiences with colleagues throughout North America, by way of formal conference presentations and informal discussions.

Scott Horton, B.Ed., is assistant principal at Ross Sheppard High School in Edmonton, Alberta.

Reading Our Students: A Foundation for Meaningful Assessment

by Brent McKeown and Scott Horton

CONTENTS

> Do not dictate to your author; try to become him. Be his fellow-worker and accomplice. If you hang back, and reserve and criticize at first, you are preventing yourself from getting the fullest possible value from what you read. But if you open your mind as widely as possible, then signs and hints of almost imperceptible fineness, from the twist and turn of the first sentences, will bring you into the presence of a human being unlike any other. (Woolf, 2002, p. 262)

Consider a possible paraphrase of Woolf's famous words:

> Do not dictate to your *student*; try to become him. Be her fellow-worker and accomplice. If you hang back, and reserve and criticize at first, you are preventing yourself from getting the fullest possible *potential* from *your student.* But if you open your mind as widely as possible, then signs and hints of almost imperceptible fineness, from the twist and turn of the *first lessons,* will bring you into the presence of a human being unlike any other.

This re-envisioning of Woolf's famous words will be familiar to any teacher who has struggled with the contradictions inherent to teaching within an assessment framework that is too narrow to appreciate the complexities of the learning process. As two English teachers in large urban high schools who engage with students and the system through multiple roles, including departmental leadership, we are afforded the opportunity to speak with students about the different ways English is presented to them. Too often these conversations have been extremely disheartening. Students equate English class with worksheets and study guides rather than with a genuine love for language and literature.

This is our story, and it is a story born of a profound personal and professional need. We are both teachers who are passionate about our subject and our students, yet for all the professional success and personal satisfaction that our jobs have brought us, there always seemed to be something missing. That "something" was an assessment framework that fit with our professional ideals about what it means to be a teacher. Too often we found ourselves in situations where so much of the good work that we did in the classroom was at odds with the often rigid and short-sighted assessment systems that we, and so many of our colleagues, felt chained to. But if there were chains, they were really only chains of our own devices, locked through our lack of courage and conviction. We set out to change things by devising an assessment system that spoke to our students and ourselves in a meaningful and deeply personal way. We want to share our story because we believe that ultimately it is up to teachers to use their own professional autonomy to make meaningful change at the classroom level.

"The basic premise behind our assessment system is a simple one: to balance the achievement of the specific course outcomes . . . with a genuine love of learning, language, and literature."

This has been the most exhilarating, and exhausting, year of our professional careers. Surprisingly, the process itself became our most powerful teaching tool, and our students soon recognized that they were in the midst of a living, breathing research project. Having identified the need for a meaningful assessment system, we set out to devise a learning structure that reflected our core values and goals, including a transparent and involved process for our students and ourselves. The year included moments of genuine inspiration as well as wandering down some dark alleys. Our students saw us struggling with assessment on a day-to-day basis and they, too, were actively engaged in these struggles. What follows is a brief summary of the process we engaged in, as well as the basic components of the assessment system we devised.

Beginnings

In early August 2004, we spent the better part of two days sitting in a classroom grappling with the fundamental questions regarding what we need and want from an assessment system. We talked about some of our frustrations with systems we had used in the past, namely, attempting to reconcile an outcome- and skill-based curriculum with the too common practice of simply adding up grades to communicate student learning—a practice that seems to punish students for lack of skill early on and does not allow for the recognition of the vast growth over the course of a semester. We reflected on some of the ideals we had explored through our own reading and research on assessment, going back to our preprofessional years. At the end of these two days, we came up with a basic framework to serve as our starting point for all of our classes. We were also scheduled to team-teach two grade 11 International Baccalaureate (IB) English classes, and we viewed our experience with these classes as being the cornerstone of our structure.

The basic premise behind our assessment system is a simple one: to balance the achievement of the specific course outcomes, the most fundamental purpose of any course, with a genuine love of learning, language, and literature. The Alberta provincial government provides us with detailed documents, built around five general learner outcomes that actually state exit outcomes for the course (Figure 1). These guide us in planning ways to help our students demonstrate their ability to achieve these course outcomes, hopefully at very high levels. There are three major components to our course structure: Windows, Foundations, and Projects.

Figure 1 ▼

Curricular Outcomes

Every English course at the high school level is constructed around the following five general learner outcomes:

Students will listen, speak, read, write, view, and represent to . . .

General Outcome 1   Explore thoughts, ideas, feelings, and experiences.

General Outcome 2   Comprehend literature and other texts in oral, print, visual, and multimedia forms, and respond personally, critcially, and creatively.

General Outcome 3   Manage ideas and information.

General Outcome 4   Create oral, print, visual, and multimedia texts, and enhance the clarity and artistry of communication.

General Outcome 5   Respect, support, and collaborate with others.

Component 1: Windows

The Windows assignments are designed to allow students the opportunity to enjoy a meaningful and engaging culminating learning task at regular intervals in the course. Approximately every five to seven classes, our students would do a Windows assignment that reflects the ideas and skill sets they have been developing over the previous two to three weeks. Why call them *Windows*? (This is actually a question that we ask all of our students in our course outlines, and some of them have even done a Windows assignment where they explore the nature of Windows.) As a metaphor for some of the tasks that we do in an English class, think of this: if you look outside a window during the day, you will see a clear picture of what is outside, but if you keep standing there until the sun goes down, eventually the window starts

Figure 2 ▼

EFFECTIVE COMMUNICATION

5 Evidence chosen to support ideas is consistently convincing and works to strengthen the overall impression. There is a consistently seamless connection between the intended purpose and the choice of form. The student demonstrates advanced ability to control a range of forms. The intended purpose is consistently clearly communicated.

4 Evidence chosen to support ideas is consistently convincing and works to strengthen the overall impression. There is a consistently strong connection between the intended purpose and the choice of form. The student demonstrates the ability to control a range of forms. The intended purpose is consistently clearly communicated.

MEANINGFUL PRODUCT

5 Consistently insightful exploration of the given topics. Assignments consistently represent a culmination of the work and strategies used in prior classes. The student has engaged in independent inquiry beyond the confines of the classroom. The student clearly demonstrates that the completed assignments and the creation process itself are meaningful both to the student and the audience.

4 Consistently thoughtful exploration of the given topics. Assignments consistently represent a culmination of the work and strategies used in prior classes. The student has engaged in independent inquiry beyond the confines of the classroom. The student shows an understanding of how process and product can be meaningful both to the student and the audience.

ENGLISH 20IB
WINDOWS REFLECTIONS

Please take a few moments to read the comments and marks that your team has written on your first four Windows assignments. Check off each assignment as you read the comments, and offer a self-assessment using the Windows Rubric.

#1 _____
#2 _____
#3 _____
#4 _____

a) Based on the feedback you have received, list at least two things that you think you have done well on your Windows assignments so far.

1.

2.

b) Based on the feedback you have received, list at least two things that you think you could improve on in future Windows assignments.

1.

2.

Based on the feedback you have received and using the Windows Marking Rubric as a guide, how do you think you are doing overall on your Windows assignments:

Meaningful Product	1	2	3	4	5
Effective Communication	1	2	3	4	5

Rationale:

turning into a mirror. That combination of looking in and looking out speaks to what we hope our students will experience with every assignment, project, activity, and discussion within this assessment framework.

These assignments take various forms, but they characteristically feature two or three parts to them. Typically, students will be asked to complete these assignments in a week's time, although there may be times when the depth and complexity of the assignment requires more or less time. They are essentially culminating minor assignments that provide a regular answer to the question, How do we know what our students have learned?

Students receive feedback in various ways depending on the nature of the assignment. In some cases, we use existing common rubrics for the personal and critical writing assignments established by the government. Sometimes we design task-specific rubrics and include commentary on specific areas of the assignment. Ultimately, however, we offer a holistic assessment of how each student is progressing in their Windows assignments, and for this we developed a Windows-specific rubric based on the needs of our classroom, as mandated by the provincial curriculum. We do these assessments just prior to each reporting period, so that the grades represent the most recent progress made by the student in these assignments. Our teacher assessments are preceded by the students' self-assessments, which allow them the opportunity to actively reflect on their own learning processes.

Component 2: The Foundations Workshop

The Foundations Workshop was designed as a way to address the powerful learning moments in our classrooms that often are not reflected in the transition from student performance to a number grade. While building on both the general and specific provincial course outcomes, we attempted to refine them in such a way that we—as well as students and parents—can look at learning progress in discrete areas of the course.

Figure 3a ▼

Figure 3b ▼

The Foundations Workshop takes the initial form of a tracking sheet in which students track their own progress in each of these areas while we do the same.

Figure 4 ▼

At regular intervals, as with the Windows, we offer a holistic assessment based on the student's progress in each of these areas. Again, we ask students to engage in a self-assessment prior to our assessment and evaluation.

In the last stage of the course, the Foundations Workshop evolves into a student portfolio in which they provide tangible evidence of their ability to meet the course outcomes. At the end of the course, the results from the Foundations Workshop will provide evidence for teachers, students, and parents as to how a student has performed in each outcome.

Component 3: The Projects

"Projects are meant to be culminations of student learning rather than course coverage."

The Alberta provincial English curriculum is based on a model in which students are expected to demonstrate learning through performance. These projects are designed to allow the students to perform in a way that also shows their progress in each general outcome area. Our courses feature three projects: Minor Project 1, Minor Project 2, and the Major Project. Each of these has specific parameters placed on it, but we place a premium on student choice. As with the Windows, the Projects are meant to be culminations of student learning rather than course coverage. As such, they are not limited to a specific piece of literature or a unit of study, but rather student progress over a period of time.

All students should be able to work within our parameters to find a learning task that is meaningful to them. The structure of each project reflects the learning outcomes that our students will be asked to display. For our full-year students, for example, Minor Project 1 is devoted to general outcome areas 1, 2, and 5; Minor Project 2 is devoted to general outcome areas 3, 4, and 5; and the Major Project encompasses all of the outcome areas (see Figure 1 for general outcomes).

Minor Project 2 involves students in writing for a magazine that we created for a young adult demographic of 16- to 30-year olds who "get fired up about things." The articles should represent the incredible diversity and passion that characterizes this generation. Figure 4 describes the submission criteria that the students must meet.

The Projects should work hand in hand with the Foundations Workshop as a way of allowing students, teachers, and parents to see student progress in each of the outcome areas.

Reflection

Since we began our careers, we, like most of our colleagues, have been constantly working on improving our craft. Assignments get revised. Assessment systems get reworked. All of this is part and parcel of our professional duties. This year, however, we tried something different: we let the kids in on the process. One of the first Windows assignments we asked our students to complete was to actually design a lesson based around our classroom reading of Henry Kriesel's short story "The Broken Globe." The story revolves around a fractured father/son relationship with the major issue being the father's medieval world-view and the son's passion for science. It's a rich story, and we gave the students license to create any kind of lesson they wished, as long as they could ground the lesson in the curricular outcomes. We used this as a way of immersing the students in the curricular outcomes, while also introducing them to the basic tenets of backward design.

This was very early on in the course, and it was interesting to note how fundamentally limiting many of these student-created lessons were. To a large extent, they spoke to a rather one-dimensional experience of the English language arts—one dominated by worksheets and simplistic stimulus–response style questions. This assignment, in itself, went a long way toward establishing the need for what we were doing.

Throughout the course of the year, in virtually every assignment ranging from minor discussion-based in-class work to extensive written work completed primarily outside of class time, we have emphasized three aspects of our course structure:

1. The power of student choice
2. The importance of recognizing how the things we do connect with the course outcomes
3. That what we do in English class can matter beyond the classroom walls

In emphasizing these three aspects, we have brought the basic tenets of learning, discovery, and pedagogy to our daily classroom experience.

In every assignment, we gave our students some degree of choice. For example, Minor Project 1 allowed students to choose form and structure to demonstrate mastery of the specific course outcomes, designated by us. There were also times where the degree of choice needed to be tempered, such as choosing two out of a possible three works of literature around which to develop a topic. Initially, many students approached these choices with considerable trepidation, having likely had a very limited experience of choice in their previous English classes. In the early weeks of the class, it was not uncommon to have a student ask—sometimes politely and sometimes with barely restrained exasperation—"But what do *you* want?" As the year progressed and students became more attuned to their own passions and process of development, that question stopped coming up—students began asking, "What do I want?" This shift from "you" to "I" represents a major paradigm shift. When a student asks us what we want, they are really asking, "What do I have to do to get a good grade?" This is a fair question to ask, given the pressure-packed, grades-driven society that we live in, but it is also a potentially debilitating question in that it reduces the English classroom to little more than a circus stage. These students might as well have been asking, "Which hoop do you want me to jump through?" In this process, we move away from being the lion tamer; we put down our metaphorical whips and become the spotter in our students' trapeze stunt, there to stabilize the rope as opposed to carrying them over it.

Once students made the jump from "you" to "I," they began to take ownership of their own learning process and started to ask this question: What do I need to do to be able to demonstrate that I can achieve this course outcome? Students began to become aware not only of *what* they were doing, but *why* they were doing it. In her reflective letter at the beginning of her final Foundations Portfolio, one of our students wrote eloquently about this paradigm shift:

> I noticed this was the only English class I have ever taken where I was aware of the skills I was learning . . . Anyway, what I remember most about [her previous English class], was that whenever [her previous English teacher] gave us an assignment, she would tell us what to include and what not to include. She always gave us our assignments, and we never had anything called a minor or major project where we were given almost no restrictions, where we had to use our imaginations.

Another student wrote the following:

> The thing that separates this class from others is that there really isn't any "read this and answer these 50 questions" type of assignments where you wonder what your (sic) accomplishing besides keeping yourself from

"But what do you want?"

failing. After reflecting back on my work it's really clear that each and every assignment has its own piece in puzzle, or brick in a foundation. The foundation we create in English 20-1 gives us something to build on for English 30-1. I can go further with this metaphor and say that the purpose every year preceding this one was to build a foundation for the next year until ultimately we graduate and decide what we want to do next.

Now, admittedly, we have been engaged in a process—the complete restructuring of our assessment system—that is far from the norm in every classroom, but we are convinced that the basic building blocks of this process are present in every classroom. While we may not all be revising our entire assessment system, certainly most of us are consistently tweaking that system. If we are not creating completely new assignments each and every day, we are surely making adjustments that will serve our students and our profession better in the long and short term. It is important to remember that we are not talking about a complete change in classroom practice, but instead we have established a pedagogical framework that should celebrate the great things that happen in classrooms every day. Throughout this year, we asked our students to approach everything with an open, but critical, mind. We wanted them to tell us when something simply did not work, and they did. They were engaged and invested in the success of this course, and they were actively working to make it better. This is a process that every teacher could engage in, ranging from minor assignments to major elements of course design.

Throughout the course of the year, we—our students and ourselves—would recognize flaws in our methodology that sent us back—literally, in some cases—to the drawing board. Have we designed the perfect assessment system? Absolutely not, but it is a system that gets better with every set of revisions and with every bit of input our students bring to us. The very process of involving our students in establishing a framework for meaningful change has been a tremendous learning opportunity for them. It has taken some humility on our part and some faith on our students' part, as we discarded the mask of assessment expertise that so many of us wear to cover our own uncertainty and insecurity. By doing so, however, we have opened up a wider range of teaching and learning experience in our classroom.

Consider the following passage from Grant Wiggins' seminal text, *Assessing Student Performance: Exploring the Purpose and Limits of Testing* (1993), in which the author explores the etymology of the word *assess*:

> Assess is a form of the Latin verb assidere, to "sit with." In an assessment, one "sits with" the learner. It is something we do with and for the student, not something we do to the student. The person who "sits with you" is someone who "assigns

value" - the "assessor" (hence the earliest and still current meaning of the word, which relates to tax assessors). But interestingly enough, there is an intriguing alternative meaning to that word, as we discover in The Oxford English Dictionary: this person who "sits beside" is one who "shares another's rank and dignity" and who is "skilled to advise on technical points." (p. 14)

By inviting our students into the building process of the assessment relationship, we are not only building a more egalitarian base for the student-teacher relationship, but introducing our students to the concept of free, yet focused, inquiry that is at the heart of all genuine research. By letting our students into our own teaching lives, we teach them how to ask real questions and demand real answers. If we present our classrooms as living and growing entities that are shaped by constant reflection, we inspire our students to view their lives, both in and out of the classroom, in the same way. We talk to our students about metacognition as a means of further exploring the way reflection can shape our practice. We show them that reflection has real-world applications, which has far-ranging implications for the English classroom.

If we ask our students to come with us on a journey to discovering a better assignment or a better classroom, it is not such a stretch to ask them to explore a work of literature with a sense of genuine possibility, rather than—as is too often the case—resigned expectation.

"By letting our students into our own teaching lives, we teach them how to ask real questions and demand real answers."

We can teach by modeling and kindling in our students an authentic sense of discovery that will serve them equally well in their study of literature and other disciplines as it will in their study of life. Ultimately, it is up to us to be thoughtfully fearless in our professional practice. If we are not prepared to ask ourselves the most difficult questions about our own practice—and do so with full transparency—we cannot claim to be meaningful guides to our students as they set about developing their own practice as scholars.

The introduction to one of our students' final Foundations Portfolio reflects our success. She eloquently articulates the connection between the power of the process, the learning that results, and the long-term possibilities.

The following portfolio is a representation of the long hard stressful struggle that this course has been. So after all of this: what have I learned? I think that I have gained a lot in taking this class. In previous years, I was given very specific outlines on what would and would not be accepted in an English course: use this format to write about this and this, and use these examples to support your thesis or else . . . suspense music. I found that I would do well in these classes only when I followed these instructions and noticed that if I were to stray from this formula, I was penalized. Other teachers forced me to write like a square, not allowing me to express what I thought about certain pieces of literature. However, this course has been like a breath of fresh air for me. You not only encouraged, but demanded, that I think outside of the box, instead of focusing on structure or what you thought were important details, I was allowed to communicate the feelings that I had towards the text; how I had connected with it. This course has ultimately broadened my horizons and has taught me that there is no one way to look at a piece of literature.

Let us end where we began, with Virginia Woolf's *How Should One Read a Book*: "The only advice, indeed that one person can give another about reading is to take no advice, to follow your own instincts, to use your own reason, to come to your own conclusions" (Woolf, 2002, p. 262).

When we read our students, we inherit a responsibility to read them well. We have a professional obligation to use our learning and professional judgment to speak to our students' needs and desires. As is the case with literary texts, students are equally as diverse from desk to desk, row to row, class to class, and year to year. Our original goal was to develop an assessment framework that spoke to the diversity in needs and desires of each student. As a result of our work, we have discovered that the specific steps and outcomes of our process are not as important as the process itself. We are not asking teachers to necessarily adopt our structures, but rather to recognize the power of the process and to engage with their students to discover an assessment system that remains true to the ideals at the heart of all teaching and education. It is our fervent hope that the passion we have for learning, language, and literature will inspire our colleagues and our students to find their way to an assessment system that speaks to students both in and beyond the classroom and will remain with them throughout their lives.

References

Wiggins, G. (1993). *Assessing student performance: Exploring the purpose and limits of testing.* San Francisco: Jossey-Bass.

Woolf, V. (2002). How should one read a book? In K. Evans, L. Farren, D. Friend, J. Hannaford, S. Poyntz, J. Robson, et al. (Eds.), *Imprints 12* Volume 2 (pp. 261–270). Toronto, ON: Gage Learning Corporation.

Holly Clark Tornrose

Holly Clark Tornrose, B.A., M.A.T., C.A.S., teaches English at Yarmouth High School in Yarmouth, Maine. Holly enjoys gardening, yoga, golf, writing, reading, and spending time with her husband and her dog in the mountains of Maine.

Collect, Select, Reflect: Effective Use of Portfolios in the Classroom

by Holly Clark Tornrose

How does supporting students in collecting, selecting, and reflecting on their work improve student learning?

Like many English teachers, I was familiar with the idea of keeping portfolios with students when I took a position at Yarmouth High School and learned of the Writing Assessment Portfolio that had been developed by the English teachers and had been in place for several years at the school. The Writing Assessment Portfolio is a collection of five specific pieces of writing from each year of high school. By graduation time, a student's portfolio would demonstrate his or her ability to write competently for a variety of purposes. In this way, the portfolio is most similar to, but not fully, a "learning goals portfolio."

> "[A portfolio] organized to show how well students are able to meet the learning goals of a particular grade level and subject area." (Davies, 2011, p. 82)

> It is not fully a learning goals portfolio since the Writing Assessment Portfolio is a slice of student writing not accompanied by "an explanation of how each piece of work addresses the goal." (Davies, 2011, p. 82)

During my time at Yarmouth High School, the English Learning Area identified seven content standards, or what our district refers to as *essential learnings:* Reading Process, Literary Analysis, Language Development, Research Process, Oral

Communication, Writing Process, and Standard English Conventions. The essential learnings, or learning targets, are closely aligned with the Maine State Learning Results. The Writing Assessment Portfolios keyed in on two of these seven essential learnings: Writing Process and Standard English Conventions. Toward the end of the school year, after the students had collected this work, the English department scored the portfolios collectively and holistically with a rubric to determine the degree to which students were meeting the standard for writing.

In order to assist students in keeping their work for the Writing Assessment Portfolio, I had them collect all their written work in a manila folder kept in the classroom. This included writing samples and major assessments that targeted any of the seven essential learnings. I called this their classroom portfolio. It was a loose collection of their work with little organization, clear purpose, or formalized reflection. As the end of the year approached, students selected the final draft of one of each of the five specific kinds of writing required at their grade level to put into their Writing Assessment Portfolio. For example, my sophomore students were asked to compile a book review, a writing-on-demand narrative piece, a resume, a quote reflection, and a research paper.

"The core of my frustrations surfaced. I had multiple (and conflicting) purposes for portfolios taking place within my classroom."

I found this process difficult when, toward the close of the school year, I asked students to pull one of each of the five specific writing assignments for their Writing Assessment Portfolios. Some had chosen samples that they considered to be their best quality, or of which they were most proud, but which were not one of the five specific assignments determined by the department, and therefore could not be put into the Writing Assessment Portfolio. In effect, the system we had created required teachers to tell students that they could not put the samples that students felt demonstrated their best writing into the portfolio, even though the purpose of the Writing Assessment Portfolio was to assess whether students had met the learning goals in writing for a particular grade level. The students felt we weren't fully valuing what they considered their best writing. I was determined to figure out what wasn't working for me with the use of portfolios in my classroom and to resolve what issues I could.

Through a university assessment course at the University of Southern Maine and some ongoing professional development in our district (with Dr. Anne Davies as instructor and critical friend), the core of my frustrations surfaced. I had multiple (and conflicting) purposes for portfolios taking place within my classroom. In fact, I had two purposes: (a) to collect their finished writing in order to select a slice of student work in five specific areas of writing for the Writing Assessment Portfolio and (b) to collect work in all areas of class, over time, to look for growth and to value the complete range of student work in my class. I was also frustrated because I was implementing a system that had little emphasis on student choice in the selection of work for the Writing Assessment Portfolio and did not ask students to reflect on the work they selected to demonstrate their skills in Writing Process or Standard English Conventions. I also did not have a process for looking at the work collected in the classroom portfolio beyond the end-of-the-year process. The path then became clear to me:

1. I had to be clear about which purpose I wanted to prioritize and to clarify this in my portfolio system with my students;

2. I had to create opportunities for selection and reflection within the classroom portfolio, other than the pulling of written work for the Writing Assessment Portfolio at the close of the year.

Figure 1 ▼

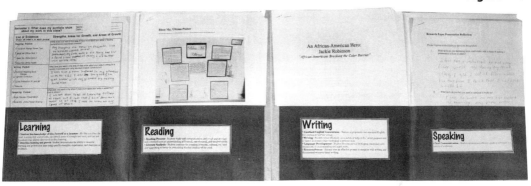

During my summer assessment course, I developed a portfolio system for the next school year that would both capture the process of student learning in multiple areas and allow students to see growth over time, since I felt that this was my key purpose for collecting student work. I wanted students to be able to see and appreciate their growth, not just in writing-related learning goals but in other areas of our class as well.

For example, some students photographed their posters and wrote reflections, such as the following:

> *There is more to this picture than you can see. This is a photo of my poster for my Bless me, Ultima project. My thesis statement was, "Antonio has a rough life that is comparable to an ever going up roller coaster. His voyage to maturity is overflowing with countless events that no typical child would ever go through. Antonio experiences, illness, deaths and severe family problems. Although he experiences lots of dilemmas, they all help him to grow up to be an enlightened young man who knows right from*

wrong." In terms of my ability to analyze a book, I want you to notice that I worked very hard on this project while learning lots of different lifestyles, especially some of the rougher ones including Antonio's life. I worked very hard on this poster and it is shown by the time taken into account on the drawings and the pasting of the text on the poster. The aspect of this project of which I am most proud is the pictures that I drew on the project. Over the years I have resorted to the internet to get all of my pictures, and on this project I decided to draw in my own pictures. They actually did come out pretty good and I got a good grade on them.

Figure 2 ▼

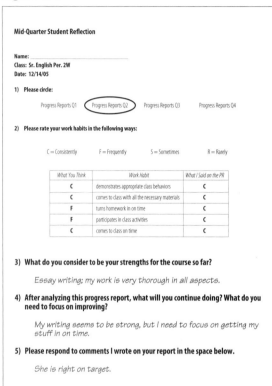

For largely practical reasons of needing an inexpensive way for students to assemble a portfolio with a few sections, I organized a classroom portfolio into four pockets by taping two pocketed folders together and labeling them in the following way (Figure 1, p. 19). I clustered together several of the content standards, what our school district refers to as *essential learnings,* for three of the pockets:

1. Reading—Reading Process, Literary Analysis

2. Writing—Writing Process, Standard English Conventions, Language Development, Research Process

3. Speaking—Oral Communication

I kept the fourth pocket as a place for progress reports and student reflections. This pocket was labeled *Learning.* On the front of each pocket was a brief description of each of the essential learnings for that pocket. Photos of student work, accompanied by a simple template that they completed to document the experience, proved to be an effective way to value hands-on projects that were too large to physically fit in the portfolio, or presentation experiences that could not be easily captured on paper. In addition, I added a place to collect documents that took a broad view of student learning, whether that be teacher-created documents such as a progress report, or student-created documents such as a reflection or goal-setting sheet. Progress reports that detailed a student's work and included a grade or mark for the work to date were shared with parents at midterm.

Figure 3 ▼

Periodic student reflections were also placed in the portfolio at the midpoint in a quarter (Figure 2). Then progress reports were written at the end of the term or at other points in the year when I felt students had collected work that demonstrated their growth. These reflections asked students to look for growth in the content goals of the class and in their work habits, and then to set goals based on their observations (Figure 3).

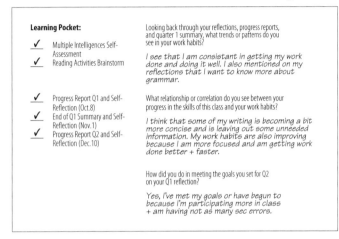

In one area of my classroom, students stored their classroom portfolios and a separate manila folder that showed a list of required writing pieces for their grade level. This clearly indicated to the students that there were two distinct purposes and processes going on. The Writing Assessment Portfolio was made up of a slice of work that was collected deliberately over the year in the manila folder. The classroom portfolio was where students collected, selected, and reflected on their work, and looked for growth.

Being a little unsure of my new portfolio process, I used it only with my sophomore world literature students. With my advanced placement literature and composition seniors, I continued to keep primarily the same portfolio setup I had implemented the previous year. This provided me with a contrast between the two systems, which made it clear that having students collect, organize, and reflect on evidence of their learning does, in fact, improve student learning in a number of ways.

Valuing ALL Essential Learnings

The differences between the two classes' experiences with portfolios showed me that my students placed value on what the portfolio system valued. My seniors, who had only collected their writing and not the other work of the class, highly valued their writing and felt proud of their work in this area. Some of them felt a great sense of growth by midyear, and many more could see the growth in the writing by the end of the year. What was, however, less apparent to them was their growth in the other areas of class: as readers and writers and thinkers about literature, oral communicators, and researchers. I attribute this largely to how the portfolio was set up, in that it overemphasized the writing in comparison to the other goals of the course. Therefore, students were most aware of their learning and growth in this area of class.

On the other hand, my sophomores had a broader understanding of their learning in English. They saw the growth in their work that year more along the lines of reading, writing, and oral communication—exactly the three main clusters of the content standards within the portfolio system. Having students collect, organize, and reflect on their learning in this way helped to keep a wider perspective on their work in class. It has also helped them to see their relative strengths and weaknesses in different areas of class, to be aware of the process of their learning, to observe their growth over time in different areas, and to set specific learning targets for the future.

"Having students collect, organize, and reflect on evidence of their learning does, in fact, improve student learning."

The overemphasis on writing in the senior year portfolios influenced students to place a greater value on writing skills, including standard English conventions, and a lesser value on our other work, which connected to the other five essential learnings of all language arts classes at our high school. This was true despite the fact that both courses focused on the same seven essential learnings (albeit at different skill levels), that all work was assessed within these seven essential learnings, and that all learning was reported out on progress reports, which categorized their grades or marks into the same seven areas.

Emphasizing Content and Keeping Work Habits in Perspective

I also noticed that my seniors were less articulate and specific when writing reflections or self-observations on their learning in regard to the other content standards, whereas the specificity of my sophomores' reflections was quite impressive. The seniors tended to make more comments about their work habits and less detailed comments about specific content areas of strength and areas for growth. It was more typical for one of my senior students to address a work habit such as "starting my paper earlier" in the reflections rather than a specific content goal of "better integration of textual evidence to support my thesis." The sophomore reflections demonstrated more of an understanding of how they were doing in relation to our learning targets and what they needed to do to get there, part of which included points about work habits.

Based on these reflections, the sophomores were very clear on what they needed to learn and also about how their work habits could better support them in this process. My seniors were less clear about what they needed to learn within the course; therefore, the use of any insight and the changes they made in their work habits would have a less significant impact on their learning and achievement of specific skills or knowledge of the course.

Increase in Self-Efficacy

Although I could recognize growth in the skills demonstrated by both my seniors and my sophomores as readers, writers, speakers, and thinkers, my sophomore students had a greater sense of *self-efficacy* (a belief in one's ability to learn—a term connected with the work of Albert Bandura) than my senior students. I attribute this to the close observation of their growth facilitated through the collecting, organizing, and reflecting on their work through this kind of classroom portfolio. I was very pleased to see this shift, since self-efficacy has a significant impact on learning. If people do not believe they can do it, they will not learn as much or perform as well within the activity. When people are aware of the progress that they have made, they gain confidence for future learning. This awareness of growth also helps to empower students in their learning. Instead of feeling that they may lack an inherent ability to master something, they see it as part of the process of learning. For example, hearing students go from making statements such as, "I am horrible at English," to "I am working on writing better thesis statements," represented a shift from making a generalization about their nature as a student to identifying a specific target area for future growth—one that a student may feel is within reach, since they have seen themselves grow in that specific area or other areas of class. This shift in attitude or belief about learning helps students to take responsibility for their own growth and to strive to do what they can to help themselves learn.

"Instead of feeling that they may lack an inherent ability to master something, they see it as part of the process of learning."

While I observed noteworthy growth in my senior students over the year, they were less able to articulate and appreciate this growth and therefore did not experience self-efficacy as I described above. They still regarded some of the learning targets of the course as being skills that they either had or did not have, and were less clear on why they may have been experiencing growth in this area, if they observed growth at all. This was particularly true in skills made less tangible to them in their portfolio system, such as literary analysis. In fact, literary analysis was an area that I felt many students had demonstrated the most growth in, based on their becoming more critical, active readers, and the greater complexity of their insights developed in papers by the end of the year, or sophisticated points raised in discussions.

It was surprising to me that many of the student reflections revealed that they did not feel a great sense of growth in literary analysis, in contrast to my observations and the fact that we had worked on developing greater active reading skills and tackled many new concepts in literary analysis, literary criticism, and specific aspects of analytical writing about literature. It was my hypothesis at this time that their learning in this area had not been made as clear because of the way I was asking them to collect the work for our class. I also was not asking them as often to select work and reflect on their learning, as I had with my sophomore students. Students could not see their own growth as easily because of the framework of the portfolio, and therefore, I did not see a similar shift in self-efficacy that I had with the sophomore students (Figure 4).

Figure 4 ▼

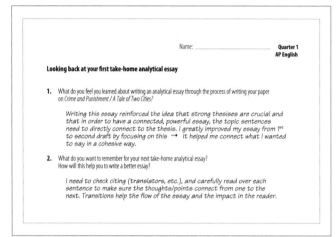

Over the past two years, I have also implemented the new classroom portfolio with my seniors. Written reflections and conversations with these students have confirmed my initial insights into the use of these portfolios because the seniors have been as aware and articulate about their growth in all areas of class as the group of sophomores I describe above. For example, when asked to reflect on their growth in literary analysis, this year's students more consistently and specifically addressed this point in their critical analysis papers. The students also demonstrated a similar feeling of self-efficacy as the group of sophomores I discussed above. In addition, I also believe more students have better met the overall learning targets for the course during the last two years. It is my observation that they better understand what the targets are for the class, how they are doing in relation to these targets, and how their processes (learning process and work habits) are contributing to their learning, and are, therefore, more successful in mastering these skills and knowledge. One indicator of the senior students' self-efficacy is reflected in the number of students who opted to take the national Advanced Placement Literature and Composition Exam during this change in practice. During the previous two years, one-third of students in the class opted to take the national AP exam. The year following the change in portfolios, three-quarters of my students opted to take the exam.

Valuing Growth and Not Emphasizing Achievement in the Writing Assessment Portfolio

Figure 5 ▼

Since implementing the new process/ progress classroom portfolio, the Writing Assessment Portfolio took on a muted role in both courses. Students regarded it as simply a slice or sampling of their work and not as the primary way that students demonstrate their learning. I have purposely de-emphasized it (except for stressing that all of it must be completed) and have kept the purpose of that portfolio clear. Unlike the classroom portfolios, the focus is not on growth. The purpose of the Writing Assessment Portfolio is to have a collection of work over time that demonstrates that students have met a standard of writing by the end of high school. In addition to ongoing classroom assessments, it is one way in which the English Learning Area has chosen to help students document their ability to write effectively to a minimum standard, a graduation requirement in our state.

Writing Assessment Portfolio Rubric

	Does Not Meet the Standard	Partially Meets the Standard	Meets the Standard
Content Development	• The aim of the pieces is often unclear • Content is often not relevant or clear • The writer often does not provide evidence to support topic development or does not often do so in an organized manner	• The aim of the pieces is sometimes unclear • Content is sometimes relevant and clear • The writer does not consistently use evidence effectively to support topic development or does not often do so in an organized manner	• The aim of the pieces is clear • Overall content of the assignments is relevant and clear • The writer uses evidence effectively to support topic development in an organized manner
Style	• Sentence structure is simplistic • Words are not carefully chosen • Writer often does not use words correctly	• Sentence structure is not varied • Words are sometimes not carefully chosen • Sometimes words are not used correctly	• A variety of sentence structure is used • Writing reflects a conscious use of word choice
Standard English Conventions	• Punctuation, spelling, and mechanics interfere with communication of the ideas	• Punctuation, spelling, and mechanics sometimes interfere with communication of the ideas	• Punctuation, spelling, and mechanics do not interfere with communication of the ideas
MLA Documentation	• Works Cited is not done • Paper(s) do not use in-text citation	• Works Cited is incorrect at times • Paper(s) use in-text citation inaccurately and inappropriately at times	• Works Cited is correct • Paper(s) use in-text citation accurately and appropriately

Required Elements

Senior	___College Essay	___Writer's Choice Essay	___Extended Critical Analysis	___Personal Narrative	___Research Paper
Junior	___Critical Analysis Paper	___Persuasive Essay	___Creative Writing Selection	___Personal Narrative	___Research Paper
Sophomore	___Resume	___Reflection Paper	___Book Review	___Personal Narrative	___Research Paper
Freshman	___Summary	___Constructed Response	___Five-Paragraph Essay	___Personal Narrative	___Bibliography

The Writing Assessment Portfolio process is also a valuable professional development tool where teachers discuss common writing assignments in order to establish a shared vision of good writing at a particular grade level. Over the last few years, our learning area has revised the rubric with which we evaluate the portfolios to better represent and articulate what we know as good writing, and to use what we now understand as more valid and reliable assessment practices. This revised rubric is a testimony to the positive collaboration that has emerged from the Writing Assessment Portfolio. We have also begun to start the scoring process by reviewing the writing assignments for a particular grade level, and looking at what could be called anchor portfolios of work that meet the standard for writing at that particular grade level.

The Writing Assessment Portfolio process has also served as a tool for teachers to calibrate with one another and establish common expectations across a grade level.

"The purpose of the Writing Assessment Portfolio is to have a collection of work over time that demonstrates that students have met a standard of writing by the end of high school."

For example, as a further way to calibrate myself with the rest of my department through the Writing Assessment Portfolio, I recorded all of the grades each of the five selected pieces earned in my class to see to what degree I was on target with the other teachers in terms of standards for writing. This was a helpful strategy for me to determine whether the standards for writing that I had established in my classroom coincided with the expectations of the other English teachers and to open up a conversation when the expectations were not aligned.

What Do the Students Say?

On the World Literature II feedback sheet at the end of the first year of implementing the new classroom portfolios, I requested feedback from my students by asking these three questions:

1. Did you like keeping a collection of your work in the different areas of class?
2. Did you feel that you had more of an idea of your strengths and areas for growth due to the portfolios?
3. Did you find the mid-quarter and end-of-quarter progress reports helpful?

The results of the feedback were as follows:

- 88 percent of students surveyed (27 of 31) said they liked keeping the portfolios.

- 84 percent of students surveyed (26 of 31) said they had more of an idea of their strengths and weaknesses due to the portfolios. (It was interesting to note, however, that two of the four who said they did not like keeping a portfolio said they had more of an idea of their strengths and weaknesses due to the portfolios.)

- 94 percent of students surveyed (29 of 31) said they found the midquarter and end-of-quarter progress reports helpful. (These are the primary ways that students reflect on the work collected in the portfolio.)

Based on this data, I concluded that the great majority of students find the portfolios enjoyable and helpful in their learning and find the regular progress reports helpful as well.

How Did This Portfolio System Spread Into Other Classrooms?

Other teachers in my department were curious about the portfolio system I was using. One of the freshman teachers was particularly interested in this work, since she had also been experimenting with having students collect their work in all areas (not just writing). She experimented with this four-pocket system for the second half of that first year and also observed a beneficial impact with her students. We brought our work to a meeting within our department to "tune" our process of implementing the broader portfolios in the classroom.

One outcome of this discussion was reclustering the content standards. As described on page 20, I had clustered the content standards into three groupings: (1) Reading—Reading Process, Literary Analysis; (2) Writing—Writing Process, Standard English Conventions, Language Development, Research Process; and (3) Speaking—Oral Communication—largely for the practical reason of the ability to assemble the four-pocket classroom portfolio with inexpensive supplies typically ordered by my school.

At this meeting, the teachers decided to adapt the process and use portfolios with seven pockets in order to work with the following clusters of content standards: Reading Process/Literary Analysis; Writing Process/Standard English Conventions; Research Process; Language Development; Oral Communication; and two additional areas designated for Learning (a place for reflections of learning in the very first pocket before the first tab) and Edited Writing (collection of final pieces to be considered for the Writing Assessment Portfolio). Brief descriptions of the district's essential learnings are mounted on the inside front of the portfolio. I was very pleased with this decision since having more specifically defined categories would allow for more observations of student learning in relation to the learning targets.

"We agreed, as a department, to send classroom portfolios home at least once a year for an at-home conference or informal sharing with parents."

Another outcome of the meeting, to my surprise and delight, was that the group collectively decided to have all of our students at all grade levels collecting and organizing their work according to the same categories, as a component of our local common assessment system, a demonstration of mastery of the State Learning Results needed for graduation.

The department also decided to invest in buying more durable, seven-pocket, plastic portfolios for students to use for all four years of high school. They were available at a reduced price (the binders cost approximately $7 and students purchase them for $5). At the end of the year, the pieces for the Writing Assessment Portfolio were collected from the Edited Writing section and put in the Writing Assessment Portfolio. The school held on to the pieces in the Writing Assessment Portfolio until the student graduated. At the end of their senior year, students were given their Writing Assessment Portfolio of work from each year of high school.

The classroom portfolios were emptied of work at the end of the year, and the school housed them over the summer in the previous year's teacher's classroom. At the beginning of the next school year, students brought their classroom portfolios to their new English teachers. At graduation, students took home the classroom portfolio since they purchased them during their first year.

Another spin-off of the process of tuning this work within our department is that one teacher did his professional-development action-research project the following year on how having students write reflections influenced their writing. He wanted to target this area in the use of portfolios with his students.

How Has the Use of Portfolios Progressed?

All members of the English Learning Area have continued to implement the broader portfolios where students collect work in all areas of class. Individuals have been experimenting on how to use the portfolios with students in an ongoing way. We have discussed and supported one another on how to help students keep their classroom portfolios organized and how to use the time with portfolios more efficiently and effectively in class.

As our school altered our formal student-led conference model, we shifted from having the Writing Assessment Portfolio as the focus for the sophomore year conference to using the classroom portfolio as a focal point of an informal sharing of student work with parents. We agreed, as a department, to send classroom portfolios home at least once a year for an at-home conference or informal sharing with parents. We included a letter to parents explaining the use of portfolios in the classroom and asked them to share with us their thoughts on the new portfolio process.

The comments from parents have been overwhelmingly positive. A highlight of their responses are:

Figure 6 ▼

Sophomore Portfolio Contents: *(Most recent at the back of section)*   Name: _____

First Section w/o Tab:
_____ Assessing Students' Multiple Intelligences
_____ Progress Report Quarter 1
_____ Progress Report Quarter 1 Reflection (stapled to progress report)
_____ End of Quarter 1 Summary Sheet
_____ Progress Report Quarter 2
_____ Progress Report Quarter 2 Reflection (stapled to progress report)

Reading Process/Literary Analysis:
_____ Blue quiz reflection sheet stapled to all of your Hamlet quizzes
_____ Hamlet Final Assessment: Test
_____ Hamlet Project and Project Rubric
_____ Journal #1 on Mid-Year Choice Book
_____ Journal #2 on Mid-Year Choice Book

Writing Process/SEC:
_____ Standard English Conventions Pre-Test Score Sheet (yellow)
_____ Book review of summer reading book (multiple drafts)

Language Development:
_____ Parts of Speech Quiz
_____ *Lesson 1:* 1-10 Quiz
_____ 1: 11-20 Quiz
_____ *Lesson 2:* 1-10 Quiz
_____ 2: 11-20 Quiz
_____ *Lesson 3:* 1-10 Quiz
_____ 3: 11-20 Quiz
_____ *Lesson 4:* 1-10 Quiz
_____ 4: 11-20 Quiz
_____ *Lesson 5:* 1-10 Quiz
_____ 5: 11-20 Quiz

Research Process:
_____ Hamlet Allusions Fact Sheet

Oral Communication:
_____ Book Review Presentation Reflection and Feedback Sheets
_____ Hamlet Project Presentation Reflection and Feedback Sheets

Edited Writing:
_____ Paper that lists the five pieces which will go in this section for your WAP
_____ District Writing Prompt with letter to parents on top
_____ Clean, revised book review of summer reading book

Bring in any missing assignments for your portfolio next class.

"My son seems to really enjoy English this year. Unfortunately his grades reflect the books that he enjoys and does not enjoy. The portfolio was easy to follow. He enjoyed putting it together over a period of time and not just, 'the day before the student-led conference.' It was fresh info and made discussing it very easy. Great job!"

"I enjoyed looking at my daughter's portfolio. This approach seems to be well organized with each piece carefully selected and tied to the State Learning Results. Thank you for sending the portfolio home—a much more convenient way to view it."

"Very impressive! This seems to be a dynamic, broad based approach to language arts with multiple means of measuring students' aptitude and performance. The aspect of continuous self-assessment is essential. Thank you!"

"Thank you for providing the opportunity of reviewing my son's portfolio. I didn't know it existed! The writing within would have remained hidden away. This way I got to sit down with him for a very pleasant evening of discussion. Thank you!"

" I truly enjoyed reviewing my daughter's portfolio. It was very neat and organized. I am impressed with the growth I see in her writing this year and her analysis or interpretation of what she's reading. I also see more confidence in her writing abilities. Thank you."

Figure 7 ▼

Student Midyear Classroom Portfolio Reflection

Name: _____   Date: _____

Looking at Specific Work

After organizing the portfolio, I would like you to flag with a sticky note the three pieces you feel reflect your best work of the year.

"Best work" could mean the piece that you learned the most by creating or work that you feel really shows off your strengths.

Piece #1: *F451 Final Test.*

What do you feel this piece demonstrates or illustrates about your learning? Why did you select it?

I feel that I read this book very thoroughly and remembered details, something that I often have trouble doing. I used to only remember the big picture and forgot all these small details.

Piece #2: *Short Story.*

What do you feel this piece demonstrates or illustrates about your learning? Why did you select it?

When we were assigned the short story I was intimidated and did not think I would be able to come up with a 4+ pg S.S. topic on my own and execute the writing. I am very proud of how this came out.

Piece #3: *Book Banning Discussion.*

What do you feel this piece demonstrates or illustrates about your learning? Why did you select it?

This shows not how I have grown as a learner this year, but over the course of high school. Freshman year I would worry about socratic seminar and end up speaking only once and I would speak too quickly. This progression as a speaker is something I feel I have done a good job with and that I am very proud of.

As a group, we are most consistent in our way of having students collect their work and sending the portfolio home once a year; however, we are not as consistent with how, or if, we ask students to select and reflect on this work. Most teachers have students organize what is in the portfolio periodically with some kind of checklist. Some teachers have experimented with having students flag or highlight a few pieces of work that they want their parents to focus on when the portfolio is at home. Others have students complete end-of-quarter and/or midyear reflections, looking for growth and setting goals for the second half of the year. Some teachers do not have their students select or reflect on their work in the portfolio (Figures 7, 8).

Following is a sample of one student's reflections regarding different assignments on her midyear portfolio, in response to the question: What do you feel this piece demonstrates or illustrates about your learning? Why did you select it?

I feel that I read this book very thoroughly and remembered details, something that I often have trouble doing. I used to only remember the "big picture" and forgot all these small details.

When we were assigned the short story I was intimidated and did not think I would be able to come up with a 4+ pg S.S. topic on my own and execute the writing. I am very proud of how this came out.

This shows not how I have grown as a learner this year, but over the course of high school. Freshman year I would worry about socratic seminar and end up speaking only once and I would speak too quickly. This progression as a speaker is something I feel I have done a good job with and that I am very proud of.

Figure 8 ▼

Looking Ahead	
What are three goals you have for quarter 3?	**What can you, the teacher, or the class do to help you in meeting these goals?**
1) Talk more in class	More in class discussions; not thinking if its "right or wrong"
2) Learn to see many views upon a reading	Have everyone express a view in class
3) Try to put a bit more creativity in my writing	Try to think "out of the box"

Current Challenges and Next Steps

These inconsistencies in implementation have led to inconsistent experiences with the value of using portfolios with all students. We need to discuss as a group questions such as: How are we using the portfolios with students so that they are a meaningful part of their learning process? I believe our next steps are to revisit the purpose of the classroom portfolios, voice difficulties that individuals are experiencing, and share strategies that have helped to make the use of portfolios successful. We also need to come to some further consensus on the ongoing use of portfolios during the school year in addition to providing a warehouse for student work from the class or the location where the work for the Writing Assessment Portfolio can be placed. It is my belief, based on my experience, that all students would find their portfolios useful and meaningful if they were more consistently asked to interact with them through selection, reflection, and goal setting as a part of their learning process.

References

Bandura, A. (1994). Self-efficacy. In V. S. Ramachaudran (Ed.), *Encyclopedia of human behavior* (Vol. 4, pp. 71–81). New York: Academic Press. (Reprinted in H. Friedman [Ed.], *Encyclopedia of mental health.* San Diego: Academic Press, 1998.)

Davies, A. (2011). *Making classroom assessment work* (3rd ed.). Bloomington, IN: Solution Tree Press.

Philip Divinsky has been a classroom teacher at Portland Arts and Technology High School in Maine for more than fifteen years. His expertise is working with students with special needs in a vocational setting, and he has facilitated workshops on classroom management and assessment. In his other life, Phil has been a professional musician for thirty years. He is the Portland program coordinator and teacher for Guitars in the Classroom, a national organization that focuses on helping teachers use music in their classrooms.

Philip Divinsky & Tom Lafavore

Tom Lafavore, M.Ed., C.A.S., was a high school and middle school teacher for more than twenty-five years. He has consulted with Maine school districts on assessment, curriculum, and instruction, and provided professional development in those areas to individual schools and districts. He has also been an elementary and secondary principal. As the current director of Educational Planning for Portland (Maine) Public Schools, Tom provides assessment, curriculum, and instructional support to Portland's educators. He is also completing work toward his doctorate in educational leadership at the University of Maine.

Creating the Classroom Culture
by Philip Divinsky

It's the first day of classes in a new school year. As you prepare to meet students for the first time, you wonder how nervous they will be and how you can help their transition into a new school and new class. You greet each student at the door with a smile and welcoming hello. As the class settles down and students find a seat in the horseshoe-shaped seating arrangement, you introduce yourself and ask them to introduce themselves to the rest of the class. And so it begins.

This describes the beginning of my first day of school for the past thirteen or so years. I teach at Portland Arts and Technology High School, a regional vocational school in Portland, Maine. We serve twenty-three high schools, with some students traveling as long as an hour to take classes at our school. Our food service class is called Fast Foods and is geared for students with special needs. These students have an incredibly wide variety of abilities. Some students are nonreaders and some are at grade-level academics; others are nontalkers and behaviorally challenged individuals. In this chapter, I would like to share with you some strategies I use to create a classroom where all individuals are respected, where students have a say in what and how they learn, and where giving and getting quality, timely feedback is the focus of assessment *for* learning.

Before we begin, let's talk about time. In our class, we spend days, sometimes weeks, creating our classroom culture. I have had teachers and administrators ask questions like, How can you spend so much time not teaching your subject matter? These questions are even more prevalent under the weight of No Child Left Behind. My contention is that by spending the time *up front* to teach cooperative skills and create a respectful learning environment, teachers will save time over the course of the year.

Most teachers have a bag of tricks—strategies that work for them to get students comfortable in their class. Here are a few that I use that seem to work for my students.

CONTENTS

Charting

The first few days of school, I ask the students the following questions and chart their responses.

Figure 1 ▼

What are the qualities of your favorite classes?
What are the qualities of your favorite teachers?
What do you want to learn in our class?

These charts are then posted in the classroom. The chart that lists the qualities of their favorite teachers is posted on my door. This lets the students know that I respect and honor their views. I refer to these charts throughout the school year, reminding the students that these charts are their work. This is the students' first experience of brainstorming criteria, as well as contributing to their learning destinations for the year.

Figure 2 ▼

Introductions by Interview

I ask students who don't know each other to pair up and interview the other person. We preface this with developing interview questions together. Again, we are having the students set criteria for the work they will be doing. Each student then introduces the student whom they interviewed to the class.

The Name Game

While standing in a circle, students toss a Nerf® or tennis ball to another student or teacher. The student must say the person's name to whom they are throwing. It is important to set some safety rules such as being aware of your surroundings, only throwing underhand, and tossing gently. If the thrower does not know the name of a person, they are encouraged to ask that person his or her name. The physical act of throwing, while saying the person's name and looking at them, contributes to remembering names quickly.

All-Inclusive Classroom Contracts

Figure 3 ▼

Modeled after Expeditionary Learning Full-Value Contracts (see www.elob.org), this is a process where the students and the teacher create a contract that states the kinds of behaviors that need to be happening in our classroom in order to have a successful learning environment. This is another way to involve students in shaping their learning destination and creating criteria. It is also important to state what kinds of behaviors would be barriers to learning and cooperation. When the

Class Contract

- Be organized   - Be safe, no horse play

- Be creative   - Be respectful

- Stay on task   - Listening to each other

- Be on time   - True value contract

- Team work   - Ask for help

- Work hard

contract is created, it can either be written out on poster paper or creatively stated, using pictures, drawings, and words. We discuss what it means to sign a contract, and that by signing the document, we are agreeing to abide by the contract for the school year. We then have our signing ceremony. The contract is displayed in a very visible area of the classroom so we can refer to it whenever necessary.

Ice-Breaking Games (Task-Oriented)

Simple challenges (such as lining up by age, by shoe size, or by height, with time limits) provide a fun way for students to learn to work together and gives the teacher a glimpse at who might have emerging leadership tendencies in the class. Other games, such as timing how long it takes to pass a ball around the whole circle and continuously trying to beat the record, or finding quicker ways to move the ball, can be added to the mix. Processing, or debriefing the group dynamic immediately afterward, is critical to the learning process. Here is where we set the stage for giving and receiving feedback. Students are asked what went well and how they might improve. We practice talking to each other respectfully, giving praise or constructive critiques. When teachers model what this looks like, students typically catch on very quickly.

*"By spending the time **up front** to teach cooperative skills and create a respectful learning environment, teachers will save time over the course of the year."*

Final Thoughts

These are just some ways teachers can create a safe atmosphere for learning and taking risks. Also, teachers establish a culture for a classroom where giving and receiving timely, specific feedback is valued as a productive way to learn and do our best work.

I would like to once again address the subject of time. As teachers and schools in general are being held more accountable for their students to achieve certain standards measured by standardized tests, the tendency to teach to the test becomes more prevalent among educators. I see the pressure of making sure that students are receiving all the pertinent information they will need to be successful in these tests getting in the way of taking the time to create productive, safe learning environments for our students. In my experience, the upfront work of creating these environments saves time throughout the year with both disciplinary issues and helping students take risks in new learning situations.

"I want them to have a belief in themselves that they are capable of great things."

A guiding question for me in this work is: What qualities and skills do I, as an educator, want our students to have? Surely I want them to be knowledgeable. I want them to produce quality products. I want them to be able to communicate effectively in a variety of different ways. I want them to be involved with their community. I want to help them gain a love for learning that lasts throughout their lifetimes. I want them to learn to work collaboratively with both their peers and adults. I want them to have a belief in themselves that they are capable of great things.

I believe that by creating a learning environment where it is safe to take risks, where feedback is valued and used as an effective assessment tool, and where students are encouraged to take part in deciding how and what they learn, we are facilitating the process for our students to acquire the qualities we would like them to possess for their future.

Parts to Whole—Whole to Parts: An Administrator's Perspective

by Thomas Lafavore

It has been four years since I have been in front of a classroom full of students, but I love visiting classrooms to re-experience learners in action. I find myself in the Fast Foods class quite often. These students have formed themselves into a working team that consistently demonstrates their knowledge and skills. They recognize their own strengths and work in an environment where they feel confident to take risks. It is an environment that recognizes that each student is an individual and, at the same time, individuals work together to complete the task at hand. Such recognition explores the uniqueness of the parts and helps them become whole as a team, but never loses sight of their individuality.

"It is when the differences that represent each student's unique strengths are built upon and used to support one another collaboratively that educators are preparing students to face the world beyond the school."

As I explore teaching and learning in other classrooms, I fear that teachers who understand the wisdom and effectiveness of differentiation forget the importance of teamwork. While a differentiated classroom helps individual learners gain knowledge and skills at a level and through a method that best suits that learner, educators should not abandon the sense of team in a quest to explore differences. It is when the differences that represent each student's unique strengths are built upon and used to support one another collaboratively that educators are preparing students to face the world beyond the school.

Another reason I visit the Fast Foods classroom is to assure myself that recent policy and mandates have little or no connection to teaching and learning. As I observe students in this class offer critical feedback to one another, as I observe them perform their daily tasks, and as I welcome their smiles, I wonder what we have done. In a world that cannot see beyond the bottom line of test scores, I become aware that recent policies have abandoned the parts and only want the whole. If you really want to assess learning, visit Phil's class for a day. In that class, everyone makes sure that *no one is left behind!*

Alice Yates

Alice Yates, B.S., M.S.Ed., is an experienced educator in French and art at secondary and postsecondary levels. After extensive studies in assessment practices and Teaching Proficiency through Reading and Storytelling (TPRS, formerly called Total Physical Response With Storytelling—an innovative methodology for language acquisition), she has blended the two techniques into an effective strategy for teaching high school students. Alice has presented districtwide workshops in brain-based research assessment practices and has organized conferences with Blaine Ray, inventor of TPRS, for New England area language teachers. She is the administrator for her school district's Foreign Language Assistance Program grant.

Making Assessment and Instruction Work in a Modern Language Classroom

by Alice Yates

I danced, sang, clapped, mimed, and chanted my way through verb charts and vocabulary lists for seventeen years. Multiple intelligences aside, it wasn't working—not for me, not for my students. I knew my students were capable of speaking, reading, listening, and writing better. The textbook approach, plus endless supplements, was not getting the students where they wanted to be—able to use the language with some ease. Luckily, Blaine Ray, inventor of Teaching Proficiency through Reading and Storytelling (TPRS), was invited to our state conference about five years ago. He offered a common sense, research-based approach to language acquisition, not language learning. At the same time, our district was asked to send volunteers to Anne Davies' Learning Connections Assessment Symposium on Vancouver Island, British Columbia, Canada. That spring and summer impacted my classroom in a revolutionary way.

It had always seemed easier to start over by listening to the latest research instead of trying to adapt the new into the old. I threw out the textbook, retrained with Blaine Ray and his colleagues, and rewrote assessments using Anne Davies, Kathleen Gregory, and Caren Cameron as my sources of inspiration. I had to ask myself how to incorporate the assessments *for* learning with language *acquisition* through storytelling.

Teaching Proficiency Through Reading and Storytelling

First and foremost, TPRS calls for comprehensible input. Students acquire language by listening to *understandable*, repetitive phrases. For years, language teachers have been using charades to avoid speaking English in the classroom. Sometimes those charades go on for seven minutes or longer. Why spend that much time pantomiming a word or expression when it would take two seconds to stop the lesson or story and say what it means in English? The repetitive structures of TPRS are deliberately bizarre and/or personalized to the class through the context of a story to aid long-term memory retention. The three steps of TPRS are:

1. **Establish meaning** by writing three to four phrases, in both the native language and the target language, where all can see them.

2. **"Ask"** a story by eliciting student responses to repetitive questions that focus on the key phrases. Interest in the story is kept through personalizing the story to the class and including fun/strange details. Cognates are used heavily to enhance the story without adding new vocabulary. At all times, question words and phrases are posted on the walls of the classroom in both native and target language, to facilitate "asking" the story.

3. **Reading** a follow-up page that contains the same vocabulary as the "story" provides further input that cements sentence structure and vocabulary in the brain. It also helps introduce new words through contextual clues. Readers with repetitive phrases and single-page stories work well for beginning as well as advanced students.

Briefly, a sample lesson would be three phrases such as: *the dog went, the bank was closed, the cat was sad.* The teacher might ask: *Who went to the bank* (a cognate, depending on the target language)*? The dog went where? Did the dog go to the store? No, the dog didn't go to the store; the dog went to the bank. Did an elephant go to the bank? No, the elephant didn't go to the bank; the dog went to the bank. Did the dog or the giraffe go to the bank? Oh yes, the dog went to the bank.* By now, there are ten repetitions of the phrase *went to the bank* in either a positive or negative format. The teacher may feel as if the phrase has been beaten into the ground at this point, but many of the students are still trying to acquire *went to the bank*.

Adding details keeps interest for the auditory students who pick up the language more quickly and for the teacher. *The dog who went to the bank, was he big or small? Yes, he was very small, super small, super, super small. Why did the super, super small dog go to the bank? He wanted money so he went to the bank? Why did he want money? He went to the bank because he wanted money to buy a super small car for his girlfriend?*

(Hopefully, the students are giving these details, and if not, the teacher has a skeletal story outline in mind.) *There was a problem, class, oh no! The bank was closed! Where was the bank? The bank was closed in Tight Wad, Missouri? Why was the bank closed? It was Martin Luther King Jr. Day and the bank was closed? No? It was July 4th and the bank was closed? Why was the bank closed? The bank was closed because it was Sunday. The bank was closed because it was Sunday or Monday? Yes, it was closed because it was Sunday.* (That's the idea—*the cat was sad* would be repeated the same way, and the teacher would try to weave it into the "story.")

"The teacher is searching for the glazed-over looks of incomprehension in the eyes of students."

A reading page that has a story using the same key phrases then follows the "asked" story. Students read a paragraph and are asked questions about the reading and questions that make connections with their own lives, i.e., *Who has a dog? Did your dog go to the bank? What did you do on Sunday?* and so on.

Assessment With TPRS

Class observations are continuous. While "asking" the story and teaching to the eyes, the teacher is searching for the glazed-over looks of incomprehension in the eyes of students—assessing in the midst of learning. A quick translation usually readjusts that look. Another assessment observation technique is to ask for a show of fingers, i.e., show ten fingers if 100 percent is understood, nine fingers for 90 percent, and so on. If students are showing seven or fewer fingers, it is necessary to stop and revisit the previous sentences or phrases in the class story. Quizzes often ask students to draw the meanings of phrases; for example, when students draw a picture of "she heard," it is usually a stick figure of a girl with a big ear and an arrow going toward the ear. This pushes for more right-brain activity and creativity, as well as fewer translations from one language to another. An example of a writing assessment is a timed writing. At the beginning of the year, students are given ten minutes to write an essay or story in the target language. Minutes are shaved off the time as students become more comfortable with the process. By the end of the year, most level-two to level-four students are able to

Figure 1 ▼

After reviewing my writing, I feel I have these:

3 strengths—

_____

_____

_____

2 areas I want to improve—

_____

_____

Next time, I'll ...

_____

_____

Writer: _____ Date: _____

Figure 2 ▼

> After listening to you, I understood:
>
> 3 things—
> _____
> _____
> _____
>
> 2 questions I have—
> _____
> _____
>
> Next time, I'd like to add . . .
> _____
> _____
>
> Writer: _____ Date: _____

Figure 3 ▼

> Après avoir vu _____ en français:
>   (After having seen . . .)
>
> J'ai compris (I understood) ces 3 choses (things) essentielles:
> 1.
> 2.
> 3.
>
> J'ai entendu (heard) ces mots ou ces expressions:
> _____ _____ _____
> _____ _____ _____
> _____ _____ _____
> _____ _____ _____
> _____ _____ _____
>
> J'ai des questions ou Je n'ai pas compris:
> _____
> _____
>
> Ma partie favorite était: (My favorite part was . . .)
> _____
>
> Nom: _____ Date: _____

Figure 4 ▼

> Home performance by _____ Date: le _____
>   (Devoirs pour la classe de français)
>
> I will tell the story, _____
> Please notice: _____
> _____
>
> And watch for :
>   Body language   Acting   Speaking French   Eye contact   Enthusiasm
>
> Home audience response by _____
>
> After listening to and watching your storytelling, I'd like to specifically compliment you on:
> _____
> _____
> _____

write one hundred–plus words in paragraph format, in the target language, during five minutes—a sign of a fluent writer (according to Susan Gross).

Students are excited by their progress in quantity, but they need to go a step further by reflecting on their writing in order to improve the quality. The author reads aloud his or her timed writing to a student partner, which allows for auditory processing. When the self-reflection is added, students focus on their writing strengths and areas to improve, and set a goal for their next writing piece (Figure 1, page 41).

The bonus to this process is the opportunity for the listener to write three things that were understood, some questions for the author, and specific feedback. The listener shares this information with the writer and keeps the reflection as listening evidence. I see my students taking their writing more seriously since they are required to reflect on it, and because they know a peer will be listening to their work (Figure 2).

My students and I have created self-reflection assessments in the other content standard areas of reading, speaking, listening/viewing, and cultural connections. The reading entry log expects students to record the pages read in their readers, along with the main idea, supporting details, and vocabulary learned (Figure 3). Other reading logs are used to jot brief notes about books selected and read during free reading time. Students suggested doing current events in a way that could be better documented and used as proof of reading and/or making cultural connections. One of the students created the format; it was approved by the others and is currently serving its purpose well.

The speaking evidence is a performance-style feedback response form to which the students recently added a self-reflective rubric (Figure 4). They decided on the criteria for a speaker in either a storytelling situation or a conversation. They expanded the criteria to indicate progress in content, speaking target language, flow, and pronunciation. The ability to be understood was the critical factor in each of the selected parameters (Figure 5).

The listening/viewing reflective piece has also seen an update to include more space for the vocabulary understood, plus a section for making cultural connections between the featured culture and the student's own culture/life (Figure 6). They also use a running log for cultural notes that cites the source, who or what culture, time period, what is like us, and what is different from us.

Figure 5 ▼

Name: _____
Class: _____

Self-Assessment Speaking	4 Exceeds	3 Meets
Content: Conversation Storytelling	Content completely understandable, no errors → Deep content/answer → Rich details → Asks interesting questions	Content mostly understandable, few errors → Adequate content/answer → Some details → Asks questions
I Speak Target Language With	Broad vocabulary, no English— use complex sentences with multi-tenses	Strong vocabulary, little English, can improvise— use simple and complex sentences with tense changes
Flow	Speaking flows without hesitation	Speaking flows fairly smoothly
Pronunciation	Accent is understandable, distinct voice	Accent is understandable, no mumbling

Upon reflection of my speaking French today, I:
_____
_____

Next time while speaking, I want to focus on:
_____
_____

Classroom observations, self-reflections, journals, quizzes, and portfolios are complemented by quarterly conferencing with the teacher. This permits triangulation of evidence observations, products, and conversations about student progress. Student-led conferences are also held schoolwide in the fall for goal-setting purposes with invited guests. Schoolwide showcase exhibitions in the spring are celebrations of goals being met and demonstrations of knowledge with evidence, reflections, and new goals for further progress.

Figure 6 ▼

Après avoir vu _____ en français:
(After having seen . . .)

Continué. . .
J'ai entendu (heard) ces mots ou ces expressions:

_____ _____ _____
_____ _____ _____
_____ _____ _____
_____ _____ _____
_____ _____ _____
_____ _____ _____
_____ _____ _____

J'ai remarqué (noticed) ces choses d'un autre culture et je fais une comparaison entre (between) l'autre culture et mon culture : (en français ou en anglais) (. . . legal issues, employment, work habits, rituals, politics, sports, leisure activities, cultural values, socially acceptable behaviors, etc.)

Figure 7 ▼

Possible Evidence of Writing in Target Language

Weblog	Poetry
Write answers to survey/questions	Short stories
Write notes or short letters	Long stories
Journals	Essays
Letters	Summaries
E-mail or hardcopy to penpal	Technical writing
Simple story—everyday life	Persuasive writing
Write a personal opinion with explanation	1-2 pages research report
Analytical writing/compare & contrast	

Type of evidence:
I am able to . . . (link ability to evidence)

_____

_____

_____

Name: _____ **Date:** _____

Figure 8 ▼

Student _____	Quarter: 1
Course: French II	Date: 11/02/05
Teacher: Mrs. Yates	Parent/teacher conference suggested _____

Strengths/Accomplishments	**Evidence I Will Share**
- Writing in full sentences - Comprehending reading for young readers - Making connections to cultural notes - Understanding stories that we read during class - Timed writes and making enough of an story so that I get a fairly good grade	Homework paper—speaking and sound studio Classwork story—listening and viewing Free reading—reading logs Cultural notes—cultural

Areas Needing Improvement	**A Goal for Next Quarter**
Keeping my binder organized so that I don't lose anything and have things so that you can find them easily.	Work on timed writes at home to increase my vocab as well as writing. At least 4–5 by second quarter.

My Habits of Mind Self-Assessment:	Always	Usually	Sometimes	Rarely
I have a positive attitude about Learning	✓			
I demonstrate perseverance	✓			
I show evidence of quality workmanship	✓			
I show evidence of time management	✓			

(Mt. Abram High School Self-Assessment of Learning)

Recent conversations with Anne Davies about the individual quarterly conferences led me to create continua with my students for each of the standards. We spent a good deal of time working on them using their ideas and the Maine State Learning Results for Modern and Classical Languages. The students suggested ways to better *prove* their learning as they thought about the progression a reader, writer, listener, or speaker makes as the skills grow. We also wanted to have documents that are more user friendly than the Maine Learning Results, which is a comprehensive plan, but awkward for students to use. Every student downloaded the resulting continua and added icons to show their current ability level, allowing them to show visible progress in each area.

The students needed to have evidence to back up their position on each of the five continua (Figure 8). They also needed an overall summary page of their strengths, evidence to share, areas to improve, a goal for the next quarter with an accompanying plan to achieve the goal, and a self-assessment section for "habits of mind" qualities. Each piece of evidence had a sticky note attached with the standard written on it, as well as a feeling/explanation about the work.

The conferencing took longer as the continua, evidence, and summary page were shared. The students and I discovered that the continua needed some adjustments for clarity. The feedback from the students was incorporated into the five continua, which made the conferencing more comprehensive. It showed where each student was and where he or she wanted to go next in reading, writing, speaking, listening, and cultural connections. The students indicated the continua helped them realize their abilities beyond looking at their grades or points. This step brings us closer to standards-based reporting.

The Journey Continues

At a recent TPRS training session, Blaine Ray talked about multilevel classes, the ultimate in nontracking of students. The idea is to have a range of beginning through advanced students in the same class at the same time with the same curriculum. It is important *not* to shelter the structures of language, but instead shelter the vocabulary, just as when speaking to a baby. Babies acquire language because parents use repetitive phrases, all the tenses, and various language structures. In other words, it works to use the past tense right away, as well as the future; for example, "Here's a red ball. Catch the red ball. Oh, you caught the red ball! I'll throw the red ball again."

*"Students suggested ways to better **prove** their learning."*

In the classroom, if the same principles are applied, students are challenged with "advanced" language structures while understanding more vocabulary as it is presented repetitively. As long as the curriculum changes every year, the upper-level students will continue to be challenged. The curriculum could be repeated every four or five years, depending on the school. It has been tried with success at another high school in Colorado, with level-one students expressing a feeling of frustration but learning more than those in the regular level-one classroom. Blaine Ray suggested that care be taken not to lose the level-one students; check in with them frequently for comprehension, be transparent with why and what is happening in the classroom, and have a wide variety of reading materials for all levels of readers.

While Blaine was explaining this concept, I kept thinking about how our small rural high school has a difficult time with scheduling, due to singleton classes: one or two French I and II classes, one French III, and one French IV class. Historically, students could not always fit in a language class because of their schedule. The multilevel language class appealed to me as part of the solution to our scheduling nightmare. Nor would students be tracked, since all students could take any French class that fit into their schedule.

Our school approved the proposal to pilot several sections of "Uni-Français." We still have one French I and one French II class this year. The plan is to compare the pilot program with the traditional single-level TPRS class at the end of the year. Our French students took the New York Regency Exam last spring, and this year's students will also take the exam for comparison data. The students will be asked to reflect on their learning, as well as the multilevel approach, in order to implement improvements for next year. The multilevel approach is being piloted here in Salem, Maine, and in another location. The school in Colorado is continuing with multilevel classes for the second year due to the success they experienced in their pilot year.

"Their conferences focused more specifically on what they were learning and less on what grade they had."

We are into the second quarter of Uni-Français, and the continua have helped play a large part in assessment that seems appropriate for each student, regardless of how many years of French he or she may have taken. Language students thought about and decided where their skill level was on any given continuum standard, searched for evidence to back up their position, and set a goal for each standard for the following quarter.

Figure 9 ▼

Crystal L
French Quarter 2
Date: January 19, 2006

Goals I Have Met:

Cultural	Reading	Writing	Speaking Viewing	Listening,
Identify and discuss connections between cultural values and socially approved behaviors of another culture	Jot down main ideas & supporting details	Write notes or short letters	Oral story sheets	Rosetta Stone lessons; understand brief messages on familiar topics
Compare literature, art, or music from other culture with examples from own culture	Weblog	Short stories	Speak clearly, make mistakes; but understandable	Understand class stories told by student or teacher
Cultural Connections log—info gleaned from a variety of sources—compare and contrast	Textbooks, magazines, newspapers, nonfiction		Sing songs	Evidence of listening skills

They *all* found a place for themselves on the continua. Their conferences focused more specifically on what they were learning and less on what grade they had or number of points on a quiz. Very few students used quizzes as evidence of their learning. Typically, they looked for work that could prove their depth of knowledge.

After only a year of using TPRS and student-based assessments, French II students are outperforming the previous French IV "textbook style" students in writing and often in speaking. Multilevel TPRS classes increased rigor in the curriculum, and the student-generated continua have resulted in gains in "ease of language" for the French I through IV students. It appears to be most noticeable with the beginning students. As the journey of melding TPRS with assessment for learning continues, I am amazed at how willing most students are to try new approaches and to take a leadership role in their own learning.

For further information about Teaching Proficiency through Reading and Storytelling, go to www.blaineraytprs.com. There is a wealth of information and research at this site, sources of materials, and links to other TPRS-helpful sites.

References

Davies, A. (2011). *Making classroom assessment work* (3rd ed.). Bloomington, IN: Solution Tree Press.

Gregory, K., Cameron, C., and Davies, A. (2011a). *Conferencing and reporting* (2nd ed.). Bloomington, IN: Solution Tree Press.

Gregory, K., Cameron, C., and Davies, A. (2011b). *Self-assessment and goal setting* (2nd ed.). Bloomington, IN: Solution Tree Press.

Gregory, K., Cameron, C., and Davies, A. (2011c). *Setting and using criteria* (2nd ed.). Bloomington, IN: Solution Tree Press.

Gross, S. (2005). Developing foreign language fluency. *International Journal of Foreign Language Teaching, 1*(2), 26–27.

Sandra Herbst

Sandra Herbst has worked in both elementary and secondary schools and is a former classroom and specialty teacher, school administrator, program consultant, and assistant superintendent of a large urban school district. Sandra has facilitated professional learning in schools, districts, and organizations across North America in the areas of leadership and curriculum. Her school and district experience provides opportunities for dialogue and discussion that, while rooted in research, are deeply connected to practical and possible strategies and approaches. She is the co-author of books on the topic of assessment, including *Leading the Way to Assessment for Learning: A Practical Guide* and *Transforming Schools and Systems Using Assessment: A Practical Guide.*

Mathematics: Assess to Success

by Sandra Herbst
with thanks to Rob Hadath

Begin with the end in mind. Be clear with our students. Tell students what is expected of them. Hold the target still so that students can reach it. These are phrases that we hear over and over again. They are easy to say and even easier to repeat. Putting them into action in our classrooms proves just a little more difficult.

But . . . how do we find time to begin with the end in mind? When do we need to be clear? How often do we tell our students what is expected of them? Won't we get tired of holding the target still so that students can reach it? These questions and others are ones that secondary teachers ask themselves.

And yet, there is no definitive response to any of them. Teachers plan with the end in mind at the beginning of the semester, the term, a cluster of lessons, and a single lesson. Describing and sharing the learning destination with students occurs continually. We are clear with our students, we tell them what is expected, and we hold the target still when we have communicated expectations to them for the upcoming learning and instructional sequences. Reiterating the expectations, the learning outcomes or standards, and the descriptions of quality occurs multiple times. Communicating them to students throughout the learning does not mean we are changing or shifting course. It just means that we have organized the learning into meaningful chunks, so that students know what is coming next. In this way, they are better able to plan for success.

One Teacher's Practice

Robert Hadath, a high school mathematics teacher, invites us into his thinking through this interview where he reflects on his practice. It was video recorded at the end of a grade 12 applied mathematics course. The students were just three days away from writing their provincial exam. It would count for 30 percent of their final grade.

Robert had been clear with his students throughout the entire semester about what the learning outcomes were. These curricular outcomes described what students needed to know, what they needed to do, and what they needed to articulate by the end of the course. By sharing them, Robert had prepared his students for the final examination—not because he was teaching to the test, but because he recognized what the curriculum was calling his students to learn. And herein lies a deliberate distinction between the notions of teaching and learning. The curriculum cannot be viewed as a list of outcomes or standards that teachers must teach. Robert could have prepared and delivered textbook-perfect lessons that did *not* cause learning to occur. Instead, Robert knew that he was to focus on the learning. Are his students learning as a result of how he is teaching? What might he have to change in his teaching so that students learn more?

Consequently, Robert has students use miniwhiteboards as a tool for learning. After sharing with students what they are to know, do, and articulate, and after engaging them in strategies to understand a concept or an outcome, Robert checks for student comprehension. He asks them to show what they know on their own miniwhiteboard. Students talk with each other, so as to learn in community. He walks around and checks their work, but not in order to generate a grade or score. Instead, it is meant to inform his instruction. What might his instructional next step be?

Robert can do this because he knows what the learning destinations for his students are, and they, in turn, also know. He shares this with them over and over again. It is always at the beginning, but not just at one beginning.

As you read this transcript, consider the following questions:

- In what ways do Robert's words and thoughts remind you of your own thinking and practice? In what ways are they different?
- What does Robert value in regard to teaching and learning?
- In what ways is Robert helping his students to better understand what is expected of them?

Listening

My name is Robert Hadath. I currently work at Transcona Collegiate Institute as a math department head and teacher; next year I'll be working at Kildonan East Collegiate as a half-time vice principal.

I guess when I originally started teaching, I thought of assessment as something I had to do. I was trying to create this kind of obscure formula of how I was going to create this grade. Now when I look to assessment, I look at it more as just finding the truth. What is the true ability of the student, and how can I most accurately reflect that? And that is something I find very exciting.

It is important for me as a teacher to involve students so that I really know where they are at during their time of learning. I think it is important for the students to be involved with the assessment of learning so they know how their standing is being calculated and how they're comparing to the outcomes of the course.

Today, I was teaching a grade 12 applied mathematics class. It is just before the final provincial exam. What we were going over was actually something we had covered earlier in the year and needed some refreshment on before the exam that was just a few days away.

We did a review of vectors. There was a time when my students struggled quite a bit with that concept. The students signaled to me that they thought they were "good to go." We had gone through this quite a bit and now, right before the exam, we were just going to double-check and make sure that everything was in order.

I incorporate those kind of individual miniwhiteboards so that all students are given some kind of a voice and we could use the whiteboard as signals. It is a way to get students interacting with me as the teacher. I could get a good sense of where their thinking was at and how they were basically dealing with the content as we moved along.

What I noticed when I was walking around, and as I looked at everyone's work, was that we needed to make sure that a vector has both sides and direction. We had established this earlier, and I had reminded them that it was going to be necessary when they were doing this on the exam.

"What is the true ability of the student, and how can I most accurately reflect that?"

So, with our assessment earlier on, at the beginning of this lesson, a lot of my students held up signals that they were "good to go." Just walking around, we found a few struggles with things that we had identified earlier that were very important criteria to getting these questions right. This isn't something that we could assume that we were good with.

Basically, as I'm teaching the content in the course, I do it outcomes based. It's a bit easier in math. So whenever I'm teaching a topic or a lesson, I relate it directly to the outcome. I go through examples of what that outcome looks like, the criteria that we're looking for when we're covering those outcomes, and make sure that the students have a good idea what that's going to look like as we work through it. So, with the miniwhiteboard, we compare what they're doing to those criteria, and in the end, when it's time to be assessed, the final assessment of learning is based by outcome so they can see the direct correlation between what they were learning, how they were learning it, and what they were being assessed on in the end.

When students know what's expected of them and they know where those goals are and what they need to do to be successful, they are more likely to achieve it. They buy in a little bit better. I've even had comments from students that because of looking at outcomes and by giving them second chances to show learning, that a lot of them have been successful where they otherwise wouldn't have been.

It has been rewarding because I've had some students who have mentioned to me how they would not have been successful with a precalculus grade 12 class. In grades 10 and 11, they didn't think they were going to make it. But with the change in approach to assessment, there were those opportunities—everything was linked to the outcomes or opportunities for second chances—to really help the students know what it was they needed to do to improve and then giving them a chance to do that. There was a student who ended up excelling with the outcomes in the course and I think on the provincial exam scored in the high 80s. She made the comment that she didn't think she was going to even get through grade 12 precalculus math. So with just that kind of change in the approach to how they were assessed, she was able to find success and really learn.

The Power of Preparation

Whether you teach mathematics or not, Robert's words remind us of the importance of deliberate and thoughtful preparation, planning, and teaching. He engages his students and brings their voice into the learning. Robert could ask for students to raise their hands to offer responses; he could ask them to put their thumbs up or down to signal their level of understanding. Instead, he has each of them show what they know, not only to challenge their thinking but also to push his own thinking and learning.

All of this can happen because Robert is clear—at multiple beginnings—about what is expected. The review just before the provincial final examination is viewed in the same way. It is a beginning . . . to rethink, to relearn, to re-examine. With each step, Robert clarifies where the students are headed and why they are headed in that direction.

"They 'can find success and really learn.'"

At the end of the student learning, teachers judge how students have done in relation to the outcomes or standards. That is what many refer to as assessment *of* learning. Often, local or provincial/state policy mandates the way we record our final decisions regarding student achievement and performance. Whether we use percentage marks, letter grades, or rubric levels, the process begins by understanding and describing to ourselves and to others what is expected. Everyone in the classroom community needs to know this, so that, as Robert says, they "can find success and really learn."

Section Two
Activating and Engaging Learners Using Assessment

Section Two:
Activating and Engaging Learners Using Assessment

When students understand what they are to learn and have samples or models to help them appreciate the quality and what is required, they are ready to be engaged in assessment in the service of their learning. What does this look like in the high school classroom? Students are engaged in co-constructing criteria around evidence of learning (product or process), they are taught to self-assess and to engage in peer assessment, and they give themselves and others specific descriptive feedback. As a result, students learn more. When teachers examine and reflect on the work that students produce, teachers are able to better understand what has been learned and what needs to be learned. This ongoing process supports instruction and learning. It is assessment in the service of learning.

In this section, notice that teachers:

1. Share the learning destination and samples that show quality expectations.

2. Involve students and provide time and support for them to use assessment in the service of their own learning.

3. Teach to the learning needs of their students based on assessment evidence.

4. Collect ongoing reliable and valid evidence of learning to inform instruction.

6 **Polly Wilson**, a biology teacher in Portland, Maine, works with students to set criteria for assignments, using samples to help them see the essential attributes of quality work in science. She outlines how she developed ways to help students build and assess core knowledge and conceptual understandings, while giving nongraded feedback.

7 **Les Inouye**, a high school English teacher in Honolulu, Hawaii, provides a powerful account of transforming his practice to incorporate assessment that serves learning and teaching. He outlines what he did and how students responded. At one point he writes, "I felt like I did less 'work' but students worked harder and learned more."

8 **Melissa J. Noack**, an art teacher in Yarmouth, Maine, describes in detail how her students use protocols to give each other specific, descriptive feedback related to what needs to be learned and demonstrated in fine arts. As you read her account, you will be witness to the power of engaging students and using the critical elements of the discipline in concert with assessment to support student achievement and learning.

9 **Murray Guest** is a secondary teacher whose school system has been involved in collegiate renewal focused on student engagement. As he learned about quality classroom assessment, particularly the ways to involve and motivate students to take a very active role in their learning, he changed the way he taught mathematics.

10 **Cris Rathyen**, a teacher of English at the secondary level, comes to better understand student thinking through written conversation over time. As a result, her understanding of the connections they are making to the art and practice of communication supports her teaching and, in turn, student learning.

Polly Wilson

Polly Wilson, B.S., M.Ed., is fortunate to teach high school biology and marine ecology in Portland, Maine, where the ocean provides many teachable moments. She aspires to encourage her students in developing an appreciation for all creatures small and slimy. Currently, Polly is working to develop and field test curriculum that supports citizen science opportunities for students.

Assessments to Create the Foundations for Quality Work in Science Class
by Polly Wilson

What is quality work in science class? Is it essentially content based? With the constant pressure to fit in content that seems to grow every year, how can teachers encourage students to look at their work and take the time to improve it? How can teachers find the time to teach students what quality work is without creating additional work for themselves? One way to address the overwhelming issues around analyzing quality work is to concentrate on a few obtainable goals, which can lend efficiency and focus to planning lessons and assessments.

There are two essential goals that I want my science students to reach. The first is an understanding of science concepts that is reflected by the correct use of science vocabulary. The second goal is for all students to be thorough and thoughtful in their work so that every assignment reflects their commitment to standards of quality. The challenge for me has been to incorporate assessments through which students could develop and present evidence that they have reached these goals. The assessments that I have found the most effective happily do not require a great deal of extra time on my part; instead they offer students an opportunity to compare their work to a standard and to apply what they have learned, in order to develop their understanding and to build strong connections. It is important for students to recognize value in what they are learning, so I want them to be able to connect science terms and concepts to real-life situations, or to find instances where they can independently use something they learned earlier to make sense of something new.

Establishing and Using Criteria to Self-Assess

It is often difficult to maintain a minimum standard of quality for class work without putting a great deal of extra effort into correcting and grading. I have seen a significant difference in the quality of my students' work, without increasing my workload in terms of grading or scoring by:

a.) Establishing criteria

b.) Making sure students understand how to fulfill the criteria

c.) Expecting them to self-assess their work according to the criteria before handing it in

"The criteria for a good drawing had to include attributes that were not about skill and talent but about completely representing the object."

Criteria for General Assignments

In the past, my efforts at engaging students in enthusiastic and careful observations of what I considered to be fascinating pieces of the natural world consistently proved disappointing. Their observations were short, superficial, and lacked the sense of wonder or curiosity I was hoping to foster. Devising questions to evoke more thought and information from the students proved equally disheartening, despite my instructions and encouragement. The seed of a solution was planted when I heard David Macauley, author of *The Way Things Work*, comment, "you truly see something when you draw it."

In order for students to observe an object, they need to really look at it. Therefore, a complete drawing became the first step of any observation activity. Students generally discount their drawing ability and are apprehensive about putting pencil to paper. To alleviate their anxieties, the criteria for a good drawing had to include attributes that were not about skill and talent but about completely representing the object. The criteria for a good drawing were designed around attributes such as "the size of the drawing must be large enough to show the essential components of the object, it must illustrate all the parts and show details about the features of the object, and it must also represent details such as textures and colors" (Figure 1). A book of nature sketches provided good examples of drawings of insects that, although simple, conveyed a large amount of information about the specimens. Those drawings made good exemplars with which to introduce the criteria.

In class, we talk about scale and how the parts of the specimen should represent their true size in relation to other parts, but since scale is often difficult for some to draw correctly, it is not on the list of basic criteria.

Figure 1 ▼

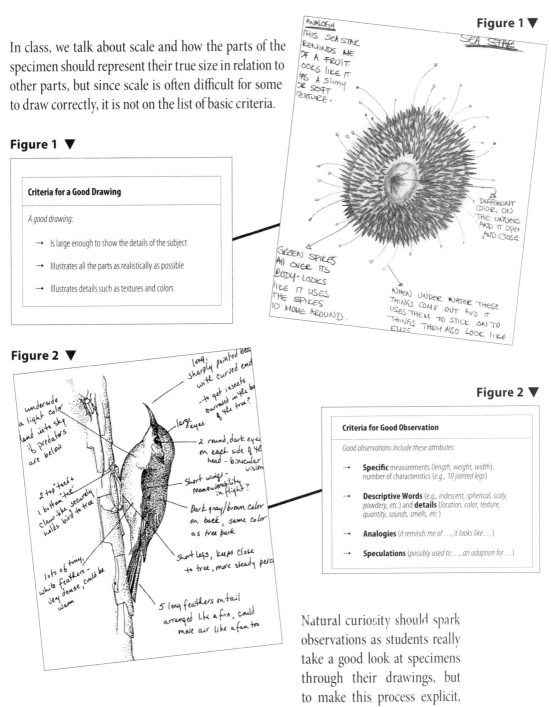

Criteria for a Good Drawing

A good drawing:

→ Is large enough to show the details of the subject

→ Illustrates all the parts as realistically as possible

→ Illustrates details such as textures and colors

Figure 1 ▼

SEA STAR

ANALOGY
THIS SEA STAR
REMINDS ME
OF A FRUIT.
LOOKS LIKE IT
HAS A SLIMY
OR SOFT
TEXTURE.

DIFFERENT
COLOR, ON
THE UNDERS
AND IT OPEN
AND CLOSE

GREEN SPIKES
ALL OVER ITS
BODY. LOOKS
LIKE IT USES
THE SPIKES
TO MOVE AROUND.

WHEN UNDER WATER THESE
THINGS COME OUT AND IT
USES THEM TO STICK ON TO
THINGS THEY ALSO LOOK LIKE
EYES

Figure 2 ▼

underside
a light color
blend into sky
if predators
are below

2 top toes +
1 bottom "toe"
claw like securely
holds bird to tree

lots of tiny,
white feathers -
very dense, could be
warm

long, pointed beak
sharply curved end
-to get insects
burrowed in the ba
of the tree?

large
eyes

- 2 round, dark eyes
on each side of the
head - binocular
vision

Short wings -
maneuverability
in flight?

Dark gray/brown color
on back, same color
as tree bark

Short legs, keeps close
to tree, more steady perch

5 long feathers on tail
arranged like a fan, could
move air like a fan too

Figure 2 ▼

Criteria for Good Observation

Good observations include these attributes:

→ **Specific** measurements (*length, weight, width*), number of characteristics (*e.g., 10 jointed legs*)

→ **Descriptive Words** (*e.g., iridescent, spherical, scaly, powdery, etc.*) and **details** (*location, color, texture, quantity, sounds, smells, etc.*)

→ **Analogies** (*it reminds me of . . ., it looks like . . .*)

→ **Speculations** (*possibly used to . . ., an adaption for . . .*)

Natural curiosity should spark observations as students really take a good look at specimens through their drawings, but to make this process explicit, the criteria for good observations (Figure 2) were developed. The attributes of good observations include quantitative specifics (for example, length, weight, and width) and the use of descriptive words to convey an accurate picture of the specimen. For example, a student with special needs created the illustration shown in Figure 3 and used the criteria to shape her written observation.

Figure 3 ▼

Figure 3 ▼

Observation

Write your observation below. Circle the specifics, underline the descriptive words, and put parentheses around the speculations.

This organism is about 7 cm long & 3 cm thick. The body is hard & looks like a sandwich (2 peices of something put together) Most of the body was black But underneeth the Black layer (Where peices have been chipped away) were metalic colors of tan, Blue, purple & green. (The agenism has to what apeers to be tiny cillia coming out of the ccloseing point of the shells, most likely used for gathering food.)

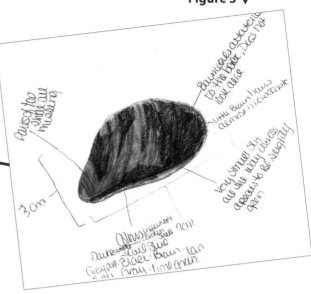

Stretching Student Inquiry

As an introduction, it is both fun and useful to have students examine something while blindfolded and offer a description, to demonstrate how to use senses other than sight to gather information. Analogy and speculation are also included as attributes of a good observation to encourage higher-level thinking and making connections to prior knowledge. These attributes also help students build new knowledge from what they already know and can encourage further research. Printed on the back of the criteria handout is an example of a drawing with observation attributes written around it to serve as an example for students.

Figure 4 ▼

Observations Include	Feedback	Current Score
Descriptive details		
Analogies		
Speculations		

Make improvements in a different color ink and hand in for a grade.

To support students as they apply basic observation criteria, I also give feedback related to each of the criteria on early assignments. This provides opportunities for them to refine and improve their work before it is graded. Figure 4 is a sample feedback sheet.

Adding Criteria

The wide variety in the quality of answers provided by students on various activities and assignments indicated a need for developing criteria for thorough answers (Figure 5). With the implementation of these criteria, it became clearer to students that details and supporting information were expected in a thoroughly answered question. Since many of them believe that a thorough answer equals a wordy answer, the criteria handout includes four examples of various answers to help dispel this confusion. Students are asked to read the answers and to score them using the rubric. Most will be able to recognize one of the answers as having many words but little substance. Reviewing the scores to these answers with the class can provoke a discussion to underscore the distinction between *thorough* and *wordy*.

These basic criteria are introduced at the beginning of the course and serve as expectations for quality work in science class throughout the course. Students are expected to keep the criteria lists handy as a reference for the entire semester. In order to encourage the habit of

Figure 5 ▼

Thorough Answers Include:

→ First sentence provides the basic answer
→ Subsequent sentences provide supporting information such as—
 → Details
 → Explanations
 → Examples

3	2	1
Correct answer with supporting information	Correct answer without adequate support	Provides too little information to show knowledge

Figure 6 ▼

Self Evaluation: **Name:** _____
Invertebrates Investigation Assignment

Drawing:

Rubric for the Drawing

3	2	1
3 views, carefully drawn to show many details, represents the organism	3 views, quickly drawn with a few details, not all structures included	Less than 3 views, little detail, not a true representation

Score: 3
Evidence:
> I believe I should get a 3 because I put a lot of thought and detail into these sketches.

Best Feature:
> The dorsal drawing is my best because its detailed and I zoomed in to show you up close and personal what it looks like.

Observations: *See separate rubric*

Score: 3
Evidence:
> I put a lot of thought into each of my sketches on the starfish.

Best Feature:
> I can't chose, they are all good!

self-assessment, early inquiry activities include handouts that require students to formally self-assess their work according to the criteria. In addition to the actual criteria, I use self-assessment activities to reinforce for my students the need for them to be able to point out evidence of their learning. An example is shown in

Figure 6 ▼

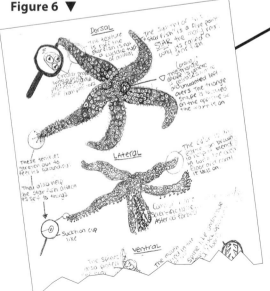

Figure 6 (page 63). Formal self-assessment is not required in later assignments, but as the semester continues, I remind students not to hand in work until it meets the established criteria. If it doesn't, the student is asked to compare the work to the criteria and make the necessary adjustments before handing it in. Along with the basic criteria, I also require students to show content mastery and conceptual understanding.

Criteria for Specific Assignments

There are two key criteria that cut across many different assignments:

- Core knowledge
- Conceptual understanding

Figure 7 ▼

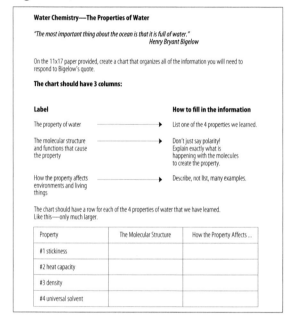

Building and Assessing Core Knowledge

Some assignments are designed to make sure students are aware of and address the *knowledge* at the heart of a particular scientific concept. Others require students to compile and organize information necessary for them to move to the next level of conceptual understanding. In developing and organizing assignment criteria, I consider what information and connections are the most valuable in helping students learn science concepts.

Two examples of this are the Water Chemistry and the Energy in Ecosystems assignments. Both give students the opportunity to organize and to make sense of information they have learned in class. The first one helps students organize their knowledge of water chemistry in order to respond to a quote that will serve as the unit test. Figure 7 shows scaffolding that I provide for students as they gather and begin to organize information.

The Water Chemistry assignment is focused on two main points that I expect students to address competently on the test: the molecular structure and functions that cause the properties (of water) and how the property affects environments and living things (Figure 8).

Creating a comparison chart is a common activity in this and other assignments, but in this case, I want students to be very aware of how organizing information helps to prepare them to speak about that information on a more sophisticated level. Students self-assess their work and then think about how prepared they are to show their understanding on the test.

Figure 8 ▼

Water Property	Molecular Structure	How the Property Affects Environments and Living Things
HEAT CAPACITY	THE MOLECULAR STRUCTURE *[handwritten diagram and notes]* The reason for this "stickiness" effect is because the hydrogen atoms they are attached to the oxygen atom are positive, while the oxygen is negative. The hydrogen atoms will turn negative to one of the ends of the oxygen atom, called polarity, and create a magnet almost and pull a positive oxygen atom to it causing adhesion/cohesion, and Surface Tension. *Water must icebergs...* Water must absorb more energy before it can rise in temperature and loose more energy in order to cool and lose temperature.	Creates a stable environment. This will affect animals who use energy to heat their bodies. Migration animals coming late, food source, industries who depend on certain migrating life. Also affects life cycle – eggs only hatch in certain temperatures

Building and Assessing Conceptual Understanding Assignments

The Energy in Ecosystems assignment requires students to organize and *connect* (diagram and explain) a great deal of information. Since this assignment is fairly complicated, the criteria are structured and clarified as detailed lists of information to include and connect.

Figure 9 ▼

Energy in Ecosystems
Concept: Understands the movement of energy through ecosystems

Task: Create a diagram that details the movement of energy through an ecosystem and explain the processes that are involved.

Criteria Details:
Trophic Levels

→ Show 4 trophic levels and decomposers

→ Show biodiversity by representing each tropic level with multiple species...

→ Indicate the common and scientific name of each species

→ ...

Energy Transfer

→ Indicate the shifting, use and dispersal of energy within each tropic level...

→ ...

Processes...

Figure 9 ▼

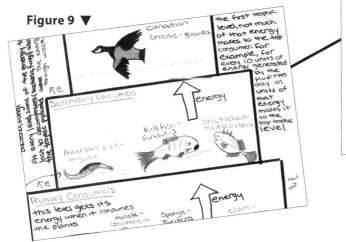

Students self-assess on the basis of including all of the required information and considering how their work shows evidence of understanding energy transfer. Subsequent activities help students acquire even more in-depth understanding of this key concept. Figure 9 (page 65) is an excerpt from the task and criteria sheet for this assignment.

Connections Across Content

Teachers look at the bigger picture of science knowledge and carefully plan lessons and units based on sequences of information to maximize student understanding. Concept A is taught before concept B so that the information from A will provide a foundation for B, but students often appear to view each lesson or unit as independent from other topics. You can imagine students locking the door on a unit after the test is completed and throwing away the key. When students are asked to make explicit connections from one topic to the next, it asks them to think harder and more broadly. In my classes, I use two strategies to help students make connections.

Putting Our Work Into Perspective

Figure 10 ▼

> **Putting Our Work Into Perspective**
>
> What topic(s) are we currently learning?
>
> *Photosynthesis*
>
> What basics do you know about this topic?
>
> *Way plant makes food/energy:*
> *. Ingredients are O_2, H_2O, CO_2*
> *. Takes place in leaf*
> *. Water goes up xylem*
> *. Uses stoma for gases*

The Putting Our Work Into Perspective activity was designed to combat this tunnel vision. It asks students to identify what they are currently learning in science class, explain some of what they know about that topic, and connect the current topic to previous topics that were already covered. When introducing this activity for the first time, the class compiles a list of previous topics to jog their memories and provide them with the information necessary to begin to form connections. I also model a connection so they are clear about the expectations. The criteria for a thorough answer might also be followed to guide the quality of answers in this activity. The Putting Our Work Into Perspective format can be tweaked in many ways and has proven to be a very useful assessment tool when used alone or when attached to a specific assignment, such as a drawing that illustrates the basics of photosynthesis (Figure 11).

Figure 11 ▼

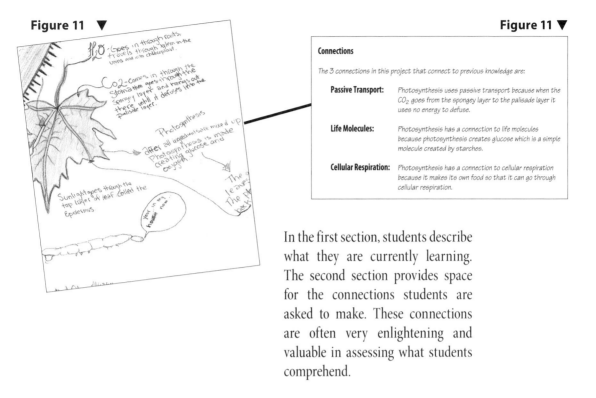

Figure 11 ▼

In the first section, students describe what they are currently learning. The second section provides space for the connections students are asked to make. These connections are often very enlightening and valuable in assessing what students comprehend.

These four questions, which I use repeatedly in my classes, have proved to strengthen student learning:

1. What is it (the current topic)?
2. Why is it important?
3. What does it look like?
4. What if there wasn't any?

Figure 12 ▼

In order to answer these simple questions, students have to pull that science concept from its lofty perch and describe it as they might to a younger sibling who asks, "What is it?" This process helps students solidify their understandings.

Try this out: Ask groups of three or four students to build answers to these questions around any topic or concept and present their ideas to the class. This exercise sparks a great deal of meaningful discussion and exchange within the groups and often creates the moment where students finally *get it*. When students provide feedback regarding activities that are helpful to increasing their understanding, this exercise is consistently cited. I find that guiding students through the process of building on previous knowledge does improve the overall quality of thinking in science class, and I am hopeful that students will repeat the practice in other venues.

Cooperative Concept Mapping

Another powerful and effective formative assessment that promotes connections, yet doesn't require grading, is cooperative concept mapping. Groups of three or four students are given handouts with a list of relevant vocabulary words and a large blank sheet of paper. The group is instructed to cut the words out of the handout and arrange them in such a way as to demonstrate their understanding of a concept. Actually manipulating the cut-out words as if they were a puzzle seems to involve students in a way that simple reading or writing does not. The teacher can move among the groups and ask questions to spark ideas. When a group feels they have arranged the words to demonstrate a correct understanding of the concept (groups often come up with different but correct arrangements) they explain their work to the teacher. Sometimes students draw arrows to make their ideas clear. When their concept map is complete, they glue the words in place and post their work. Usually one or two of the groups then present their ideas to the class. Students are encouraged to copy a map to keep in their study notes.

Figure 13 ▼

Criteria	In Progress	Finished Product
Completion __ Fish Biology __ Fishery Info __ Management ideas	Looks good: Work on:	
Connections to fish biology	Looks good: Work on:	
Thoroughness of descriptions of management ideas	Looks good: Work on:	
Own words		

Nongraded Feedback

Nongraded feedback informs students of their progress as they work on an assignment. Nongraded feedback might be offered by peers or by the teacher. Its purpose is to help students understand what is good about their work and to identify areas that need improvement. It should serve to improve the level of work that is handed in.

Feedback Sheets

Student research projects are good examples of assignments whose quality can be improved by nongraded feedback. The Fisheries Research and Management Plan Feedback sheet (see Figure 13) provides an example of a very specific nongraded feedback form that allows peers to contribute their feedback. It can also be used by the students themselves as a self-assessment tool or by the teacher. The final column, labeled Finished Product, is where the teacher makes comments when grading the piece.

Figure 14 ▼

I often use nongraded feedback on lab report conclusions because students tend to treat a conclusion as a quick review of a lab rather than taking the opportunity to connect the data they gathered with the concept the lab demonstrates. The criteria for a good conclusion to a lab report involve three basic parts:

1. Identifying the purpose of the lab
2. Demonstrating an understanding of the science concept illustrated by the lab
3. Explaining how the data gathered in the lab supports or refutes the concept

The From Corn to Milk (Figure 14) lab is an example of how students are asked to organize a conclusion according to the criteria and includes student work from a sophomore biology class.

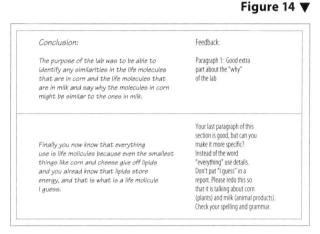

Figure 15 ▼

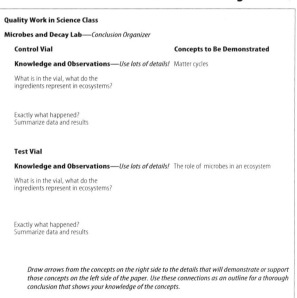

Charts

With labs that occur early in the course or with complicated labs, it is invaluable to help students organize the information needed to satisfy the three criteria on charts. Figure 15 (page 69) is an example of a chart that facilitates the organization of material for a microbe lab.

First Drafts

To ensure that students are making sense of a lab, I usually collect the first drafts of lab conclusions and offer nongraded feedback to guide their work on a final draft. It is helpful to require students to include the first draft and its nongraded feedback with their final lab report to check if the feedback and subsequent revision really helped move the student toward greater understanding. It is important to note that a few students do not act on the feedback and will turn in unimproved work. I will *not* accept this work as a completed assignment. The extra step of nongraded feedback appears to add more effort to the grading of lab reports, an already labor-intensive activity for science teachers, but because comparisons to the first draft can easily be made, the grading process proceeds very quickly.

*"A few students do not act on the feedback and will turn in unimproved work. I will **not** accept this work as a completed assignment."*

Quick Fixes

An on-the-spot version of nongraded feedback is what I call a *quick fix*. Quick fixes serve to encourage the habit of making improvements to what students might already consider finished work. Students are directed to use a different colored pencil or pen from the one they originally used to complete their assignment and make any corrections that are necessary for all of the information in their work to be correct and complete. The improvements are made as we go over the assignment in class, and students are able to compare what they have done with the correct answers or information. The assignments that can be quickly fixed are most often homework or short class work that is scored with a minus, a check, or a plus. Students receive a plus if their work shows that they made a good or excellent attempt the first time and took advantage (if needed) of the opportunity to improve their work further. Quick fixes engage students as we go over assignments and help them to identify information that can improve their work.

Conferences

One of the most powerful means of self-assessment and reflection is for students to speak directly to their parents about their learning and progress in school. Since student-led conferences are not standard practice in many high schools, it is important to develop ways to bring the student's voice to parent-teacher conferences. The students, after all, are the largest stakeholders in their own education, so it is important to encourage student involvement. The conference preparation questions (Figure 16, page 72) were devised to offer an opportunity for students to reflect on their progress in class, their strengths in general, and what future actions they may take to improve their education in a way that is constructive and informative for parents, teachers, and students. The questions were formed to eliminate the tendency of focusing conferences solely on grades.

Class time is allocated for every student to complete the questionnaire, regardless of whether his or her parent will schedule a conference. Their responses provide very valuable feedback. Here are three examples:

"We often think every assessment must be graded or scored, but that's not so."

1. Describe your strengths in this class and at school in general.

My strengths are labs, I'm pretty good at those. I'm also really good at learning the material.

2. Describe your level of involvement and your contributions when participating in group assignments.

When we do group assignments, I try and make sure no one is left out and everyone is participating.

3. Can you identify any actions (improve study habits, participation, etc.) that will help you to be more successful in class?

I will need to improve on my studying habits. I want to get better and better and not procrastinate on projects or assignments.

Ideally the student presents his or her responses to the conference preparation questions in person at a table around which their parents and teacher are also gathered. Usually a third of my students participate. Students can also conference with me directly if their parents do not schedule a meeting. The students use

Figure 16 ▼

Conference Preparation Questions

Please answer each question carefully using specifics so that your opinion will be well represented.

1. In general, how would you describe your progress?

2. Do you think that your grade is an accurate reflection of your knowledge in this class?

3. Is there any material that you find difficult to understand?

4. Can you suggest any way to make this material easier to understand?

5. Specifically, describe how your work meets the expectations in this class.

6. Describe your strengths in this class and at school in general.

7. Describe your level of involvement and your contributions when participating in group assignments.

8. What work have you completed that you are proud of?

9. Can you identify any actions (improve study habits, participation, etc.) that will help you to be more successful in class?

10. What steps can your teacher or parents take to support you in becoming more successful?

their conference script so they are not at a loss for words. The responses often spark conversations between all the parties present. Six years of inviting students to participate in conferences have resulted in only positive experiences.

Since my school conferences do not receive 100 percent participation and students are not required to attend, I will also conduct the conference around the student's answers even though the student is not present. Parents appreciate learning what their son or daughter believes is important in regard to succeeding in class and school.

Conclusion

It is important that assessments designed to improve student learning and the quality of student work be practical and efficient. We often think every assessment must be graded or scored, but that's not so. Assessments *for* learning are *tools* to help students learn and should provide an opportunity for teachers to see if their students are on the right track before a test is taken. Students need to know how to identify the quality in their own work and to add what is needed to earn a high grade. They need to understand how to build knowledge from the tools and information that surround them at school but are often unnoticed or not apparent. Thoughtful and effective assessments help students understand the strategies necessary to learn, to show their learning, and to succeed.

References

Education Development Center. (1998). *Insights in biology: The matter of life manual.* Dubuque, IA: Kendall/Hunt Publishing Co. (Inspired the Corn to Milk Lab.)

Leslie, C. W. (1995). *Nature drawing: A tool for learning.* Dubuque, IA: Kendall/Hunt Publishing Co.

Microbial Literacy Collaborative (Community Outreach Initiative). (1999). *Meet the microbes through the microbe world activities: Now you see it, now you don't.* Reston, VA: National Association of Biology Teachers. (Inspired the Microbe and Decay Lab.)

Les Inouye

Les Inouye, B.Ed., M.Ed., an English instructor with forty years of classroom experience, has taught Advanced Placement as well as inclusion classes. Having received extensive training from Anne Davies, Ph.D., Les remains committed to the power of formative assessment and to the importance of building relationships with students. He has also participated on several teams that evaluate assessments used by Hawaii's public schools. His wife, three daughters, and two grandchildren provide a welcomed balance to a full schedule. Currently, Les teaches at Mid-Pacific Institute, a private college-prep school in Honolulu.

A Curmudgeon's Guide to the Assessment Universe
by Les Inouye

In the Beginning

In school year 2004–05, as I sat at my desk staring at a six-inch stack of tenth-grade narratives and Advanced Placement analysis essays to score, Mike Among, a former colleague, walked in and asked me to join a newly formed group, the School Assessment Liaison Team (SALT). This group would be trained in assessment practices that would increase student learning and address the Hawaii standards—a magic bullet. Not a very unique sales pitch, but I listened nonetheless. I had no choice; Mike stands 6' 2" and is a former standout basketball and volleyball player.

"Why me?" I asked.

In his most convincing, pat-on-the-back, hey-fella tone of voice, he responded, "Because you're respected and experienced. I think you'd be a good addition to our team and a good role model for other teachers." In other words, "Les, you don't have too many enemies; you're kinda old and already eligible for retirement. Besides, I couldn't find anybody else dumb enough to volunteer."

This innocuous conversation marked a life-changing moment—one that would challenge my beliefs in how students learn and transform a teaching style that had proved relatively effective for many years. After more than three decades in the classroom, there weren't many revolutionary "can't miss" methods I hadn't heard of; in fact, every newfangled philosophy or gimmick had failed to live up to its hype. Nonetheless, with the advent of standards-based learning, which appeared to be the foundation of educational thought for the foreseeable future, I decided to jump in—with at least one foot—and see what this assessment thing was all about. I had read and heard the new terminology but had very little understanding of formative and summative assessment.

Besides, Mike promised we'd be fed a hot lunch! I couldn't resist.

As a "back to basics" kind of guy, the "old school" way had been relatively successful and comfortable for me, and for most students and parents; they knew that the work and assignments in my class would focus on developing core language skills. That meant, of course, the usual round of reading, discussing, drafting, correcting, drafting, editing, revising, and test taking. That also meant spending many evening and weekend hours marking papers at home.

"Gone were the days of giving the assignment followed by lecture/discussion/ group work and the inevitable summative scores."

I wondered how this newfangled assessment thing would help improve student learning. Would Dr. Anne Davies live up to Mike Among's promises? Or would this be just another in a long line of training sessions that would ultimately prove a waste of the state's money and my time? Would the lunches be as good as promised?

In a few weeks, bran muffin in one hand and coffee in another, I sat a few yards away from Dr. Anne Davies at my first session. As I listened to this bundle of energy and wisdom, I learned how to make my students work harder than I did.

There Was Light!

After the first SALT session, I left weary. Here was somebody who kept us alert and working! Not only that but the philosophy, concepts, and assessment practices actually made sense. I needed to hear and learn more. Besides, the lunches were pretty good.

Over the first year of attending SALT seminars, holding follow-up meetings with my school team, and trying new activities and assessment methods, I saw the key ingredients of assessment *for* learning as setting clear learning targets, building criteria with students, giving feedback as the work progressed, and helping students use feedback from a variety of sources to improve their work.

Gone were the days of giving the assignment followed by lecture/discussion/group work and the inevitable summative scores garnered from quizzes/exams/essays to determine the average for an end-of-term grade. Although summative assessment information still had to be provided, quizzes and tests were now much less important in measuring student learning. Further, by partnering with students and inviting them to participate in assessment practices, students were now more intimately involved in their own learning.

My most successful use of assessment *for* learning was a unit that focused on Joseph Heller's classic 20th century black comedy *Catch-22*, an assigned reading for the 2005–06 eleventh-grade AP Language and Composition class. Students had been doing numerous timed writes and practice objective tests in preparation for the AP test, so I decided to have them develop an objective test and a few writing prompts as a way to practice close reading and gain a deeper understanding of the book's characters, themes, and structure. In addition, as a point-of-view lesson, they could experience what a test developer might consider.

After I introduced the assignment, one group of students asked if they could develop a piece of art as their project. It was a scary moment for me. I have no knowledge as to what a good piece of art is. (To me, the surf poster of the movie, *Endless Summer*, is art.) Immediately, a few key questions surfaced: What qualifies something as art? How will the art be judged? What if only the artistic one(s) end up doing all the work?

"I decided to turn over some control to the students … as long as they were able to demonstrate proficiency."

Then, with not a little hesitancy, I decided to turn over some control to the students; the art group would develop their own vision of Heller's novel as long as they were able to demonstrate proficiency for an eleventh-grade Hawaii Content and Performance Reading Standard, shown below.

- **Standard**:   Respond to literary texts from a range of stances: personal, interpretive, critical

- **Benchmark**   (LA.11.3.3): Analyze how a literary text is related to historical cultural, and/or political themes and issues (e.g. women's place in society, sovereignty of native groups)

- **Sample Performance Assessment**: The student applies historical, cultural, or political information to the reading of literary text on a given topic....Analyzes connections and draws inferences about the text based on the information. (Hawaii State Department of Education, 2005)

Figure 1 ▼

Figure 2 ▼

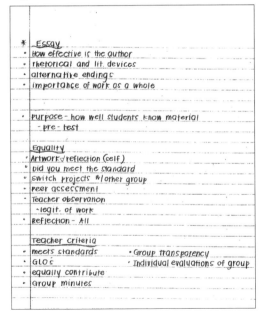

Two very distinct groups were formed: one generating an objective test with an essay question, the other crafting an art piece. Both groups were required to develop their own sets of criteria against which the other class members, their audience, could determine if the presenting group had met or exceeded the given standard.

The exam group had many models from their practice tests and timed writing prompts. They immediately reflected on past practice objective exams and remembered that questions had varying levels of difficulty. The group listed the following initial design criteria for the exam:

1. *25–30 objective questions:*
    a.) 5 easy = 80% will answer correctly
    b.) 5 difficult = 20% will answer correctly
    c.) 5–20 medium = more than half will answer correctly

2. *Have different types of questions: character, literary techniques, etc. This group also classified the questions into recall vs. conceptual (interpretive) and later determined that the test was too heavily weighted (over 90 percent) with recall questions and should have had more tone, language, thematic, and interpretive problems.*

3. *Create an essay on theme, war, time period, tone, style and diction, or literary devices. The essay was scored with a guide created by the exam group.*

Essay Expectations

- Analyze
- Refute, defend, qualify
- Author's tone, attitude, effect
- Author's purpose, style, diction
- How author uses devices (effectiveness)
- Compare/contrast

The art group encountered problems immediately. Each member had his/her own vision of what the art product should look like and how it should be done. Soon, however, the group realized that there had to be a "meeting of the minds" to successfully complete the project. My only suggestion was to find a picture of Picasso's *Guernica*, a representation of the Spanish War's horror; it was one of the few things I remember from Art 101. Someone promised to ask the art teacher for a picture and they began brainstorming as a single group, although at times, I thought it sounded like eight individuals arguing for separate concepts.

By the end of the first meeting they had agreed upon:

1. A 4' x 3' "canvas" mixed media
2. 2-D and 3-D
3. Painting and pop-ups
4. Key characters and symbols

As the art group began to focus on the visual details of their planned piece, they thought about what would be needed to represent their own response to key elements of the book; more details emerged (see Figure 3).

Both groups were allowed to do some organizational meetings using class time; however, the bulk of their planning and work was completed on their own. I made my room available during lunch recesses if they needed a place and common time to meet.

Figure 3 ▼

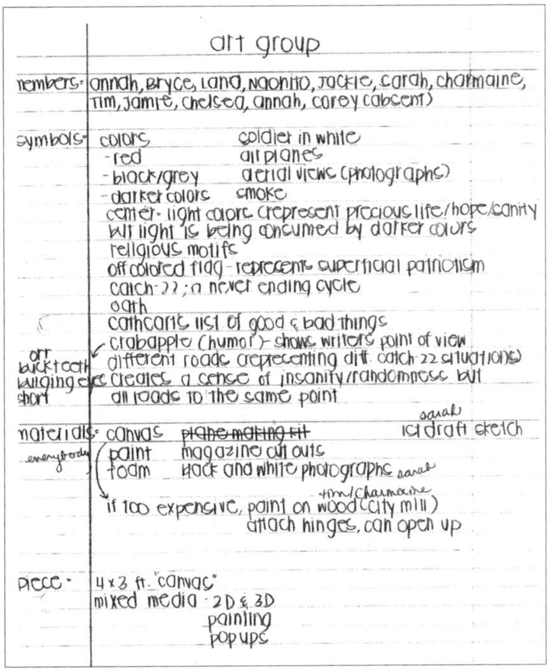
art group

members- annah, Bryce, Lana, Naohito, Jackie, Sarah, Charmaine, Tim, Jamie, Chelsea, annah, corey (absent)

symbols- colors
- red
- black/grey
- darker colors

soldier in white
airplanes
aerial views (photographs)
smoke

center- light colors (represent precious life/hope/sanity but light is being consumed by darker colors
religious motifs
off colored flag - represents superficial patriotism
catch-22; a never ending cycle
oath
cathcart's list of good & bad things
crabapple (humor) - shows writers point of view
different roads (representing diff. catch-22 situations) creates a sense of insanity/randomness but all roads to the same point

orr
bucktooth
bulging eyes
short

materials- canvas ~~plane making kit~~ 1st draft sketch sarah
everybody - paint, foam
magazine cut outs
black and white photographs sarah
if too expensive, paint on wood (city mill) tim/Charmaine
attach hinges, can open up

piece- 4 x 3 ft. "canvas"
mixed media - 2D & 3D
painting
pop ups

Presentation Day!

The exam group administered the test to the art group; the results were not factored into their grades. The peer and self-assessment stage of the project would be a basis for their grades, with the exam acting as evidence for the group's work quality. Afterward, using the criteria provided by the exam group, the tested students provided oral and written commentary on the quality and fairness of the test. The exam group also discussed the challenges of making questions of different difficulty levels, and ways that the exercise forced them to look more closely at the events of the book and consider what Heller might have been thinking as he wrote the book.

The art group presented a multimedia, three-dimensional piece representing *Catch-22's* main characters, key themes, and symbols. Soldiers' faces and uniforms were intentionally ambiguous to symbolize U.S. military action in many foreign countries, most notably in Vietnam and Iraq. A question-and-answer period followed the art group's explanation of their product. Alone, the art product was not adequate as evidence that the group had met or exceeded the benchmark. However, during the question-and-answer period when the audience asked for clarification and further detailed justification for certain elements of the work, the art group was able to show it had satisfied the benchmark (see Figure 4).

Figure 4 ▼

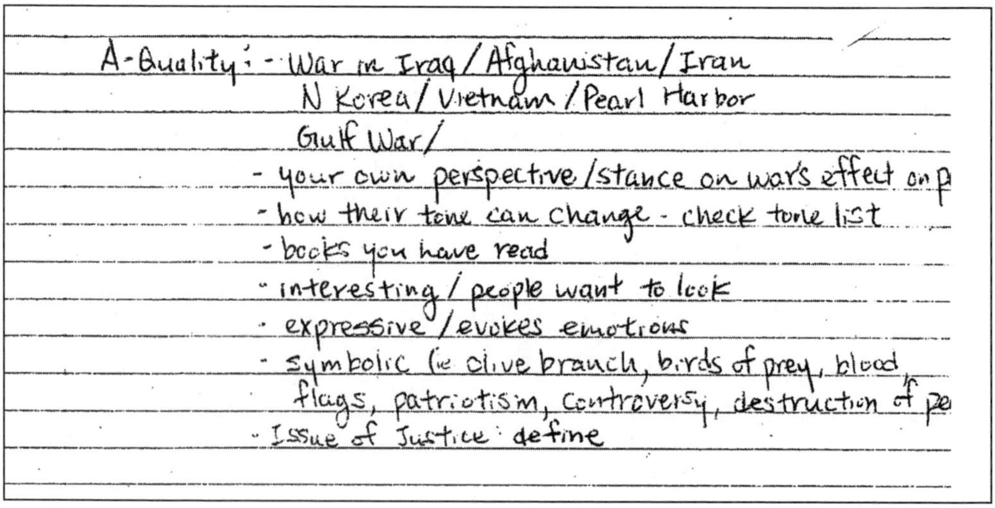

A-Quality: - War in Iraq / Afghanistan / Iran
N Korea / Vietnam / Pearl Harbor
Gulf War /
- your own perspective / stance on war's effect on p
- how their tone can change - check tone list
- books you have read
- interesting / people want to look
- expressive / evokes emotions
- symbolic (ie olive branch, birds of prey, blood
flags, patriotism, controversy, destruction of pe
- Issue of Justice: define

Peer and self-assessment pieces further deepened their understanding of the learning experience. They met in their groups and then took time to reflect on their own. Subsequently, each student wrote a reflection on what other members did, what was learned, and the process s/he went through in meeting the stated benchmarks. This reflection became a key piece of evidence in determining a final grade. A student could show what s/he had done and learned. Shown are excerpts from the group assessment (Figure 5) and a student's self-reflection from members of the art group (Figure 6).

Figure 5 ▼

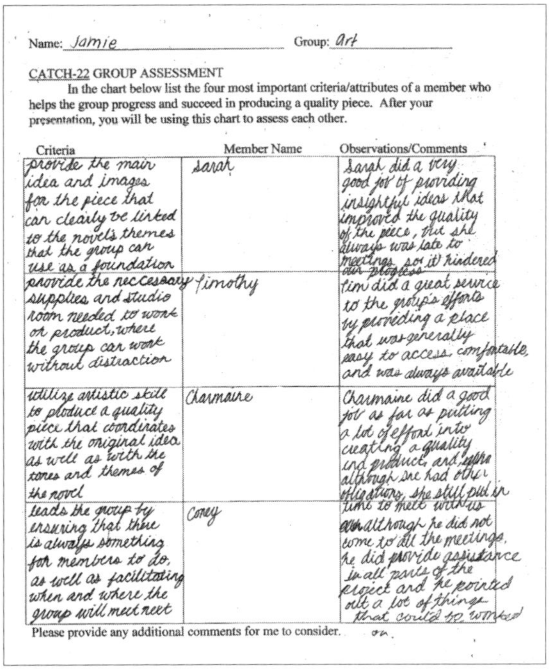
Name: Jamie Group: Art

CATCH-22 GROUP ASSESSMENT

In the chart below list the four most important criteria/attributes of a member who helps the group progress and succeed in producing a quality piece. After your presentation, you will be using this chart to assess each other.

Criteria	Member Name	Observations/Comments
provide the main idea and images for the piece that can clearly be linked to the novel's themes that the group can use as a foundation	Sarah	Sarah did a very good job of providing insightful ideas that improved the quality of the piece, but she always was late to meetings, so it hindered our progress
provide the neccessary supplies and studio room needed to work on product, where the group can work without distraction	Timothy	Tim did a great service to the group's efforts by providing a place that was generally easy to access, comfortable, and was always available
utilize artistic skill to produce a quality piece that coordinates with the original idea as well as with the tones and themes of the novel	Charmaine	Charmaine did a good job as far as putting a lot of effort into creating a quality end product, and although she had other obligations, she still put in time to meet with us
leads the group by ensuring that there is always something for members to do, as well as facilitating when and where the group will meet next	Corey	although he did not come to all the meetings, he did provide assistance in all parts of the project and he pointed out a lot of things that could be worked on.

Please provide any additional comments for me to consider.

Figure 6 ▼

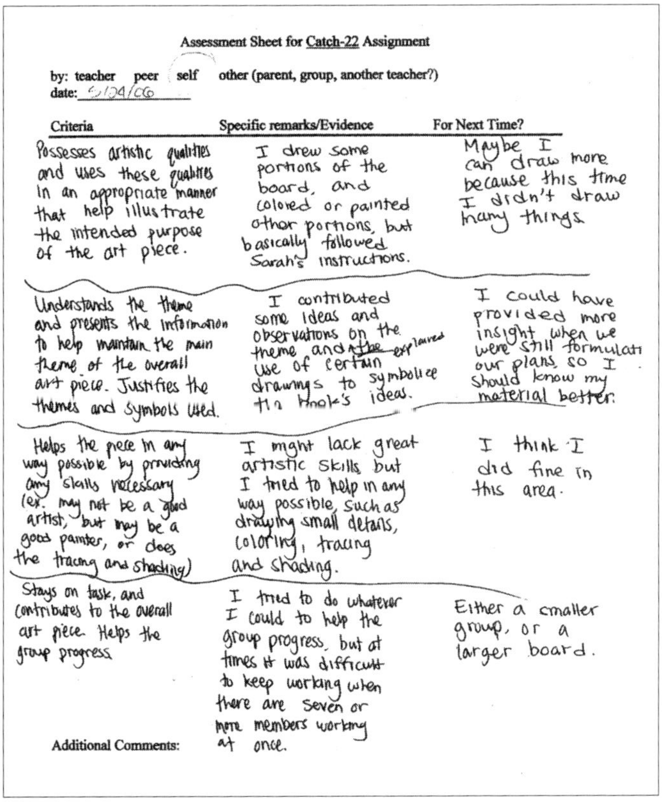
Assessment Sheet for Catch-22 Assignment

by: teacher peer self other (parent, group, another teacher?)
date: 5/24/06

Criteria	Specific remarks/Evidence	For Next Time?
Possesses artistic qualities and uses these qualities in an appropriate manner that help illustrate the intended purpose of the art piece.	I drew some portions of the board, and colored or painted other portions, but basically followed Sarah's instructions.	Maybe I can draw more because this time I didn't draw many things.
Understands the theme and presents the information to help maintain the main theme of the overall art piece. Justifies the themes and symbols used.	I contributed some ideas and observations on the theme and explained use of certain drawings to symbolize the book's ideas.	I could have provided more insight when we were still formulating our plans, so I should know my material better.
Helps the piece in any way possible by providing any skills necessary (ex. may not be a good artist, but may be a good painter, or does the tracing and shading)	I might lack great artistic skills but I tried to help in any way possible, such as drawing small details, coloring, tracing and shading.	I think I did fine in this area.
Stays on task, and contributes to the overall art piece. Helps the group progress	I tried to do whatever I could to help the group progress, but at times it was difficult to keep working when there are seven or more members working at once.	Either a smaller group, or a larger board.

Additional Comments:

Reflections

Each group's reflections on the experience revealed insights, engagement, and awareness of the choices they made.

From the art group:

> "It's not easy to create an artwork with so many artists with different ideas, but we were able to cooperate with one another to complete a quality product in the end."

> "Compared to the exam group, we probably paid less attention to the more subtle messages of the novel and therefore might not have been able to capture everything in the novel."

> "We were given a chance to be more creative in presenting our analysis."

From the exam group:

> "I know that I could have made better distracters."

> "I think I tended to bring up too many points of discussion, which took up too much time unnecessarily. Focus on only the more important concepts vs. covering everything with less depth would have been better."

> "I wasn't really a leader, but I voiced my opinions . . ."

> "Overall, I think the exam was an interesting project. I think I was also able to contribute more to the group than in a regular class discussion . . ."

*"The key ingredients of assessment **for** learning worked for students and for my own learning."*

I, too, was learning and assessing the impact of the choices I had made to invite students into the process. During this work, I took notes/recorded observations of the exam/art project. I observed that students did all of the work by consulting, discussing, and learning from each other. This discussion was better than any final review of a book; it clarified and reinforced the learning and understanding of the book. I made sure they were on task, followed a schedule, addressed specific concerns. (Hmm . . . I felt like I did less "work" but students worked harder and learned more!)

The key ingredients of assessment *for* learning worked for students and for my own learning. How often had other professional learning sessions actually resulted in what the speaker/trainer had promised? Let me think . . . hmm . . . NONE!

A Penny for My Thoughts

I mulled over why the 2005–06 AP class's work was so markedly different from other years. Certainly, the students were no more talented than previous years; in fact, one could make the case that, on the whole, some AP classes from previous years were more creative and/or gifted. The curriculum remained essentially the same. I had dabbled with building criteria the previous year and enjoyed some success with students being involved in their learning, as evidenced by more students helping each other, more work being turned in, and better essays. However, the 2005–06 year was different. That class consistently exceeded my expectations, and more importantly, their own.

For another novel, one group did a dramatic rendition based on Toni Morrison's *Beloved*, a disturbing novel about the horrors of slavery, which bordered on being eerie because of the costume design, music, lighting, and fading in/fading out speeches. Another group wrote a poem that captured the terrors and hardships of slavery. If only I had recorded them!

"Assessment practices . . . establish . . . a framework for teacher and student to communicate in an orderly and mutually respectful way."

And how their writing improved! After seeing writing samples at the beginning of the year, I feared only a few would be able to pass the AP exam. In the end, only a few *did not*, with a surprising number scoring fours and fives.

As I sit here, reflecting on the past and struggling to write my thoughts on paper, which is itself an experience of ongoing assessment, I have come to this conclusion. Assessment practices not only establish a system of clarifying goals and learning targets, but also a framework for teacher and student to communicate in an orderly and mutually respectful way. When a teacher asks students to help build a set of criteria that is actually going to be used, the teacher is also telling the students, "Hey, I think you're smart. Your ideas are good enough and important enough to be used." Working with students to help them better understand standards and benchmarks, using criteria that they have helped create, giving feedback to strengthen the quality of their work, providing some guidance, and having students set personal learning goals all take time and patience. The process does not occur in one day, but if done over time, students become more connected to their own work and are willing to move toward excellence.

Two Steps Forward, One Step Back

As the SALT teachers began using assessment practices as taught by Anne Davies and started experiencing some success, we felt confident enough to host a few workshops for our colleagues. As expected, most implemented one or two assessment activities/techniques, while some resisted. Some were just too busy.

Nonetheless, a few teachers asked our SALT team about assessment *for* learning. We shared tips and strategies. A few even sat in when my classes were doing criteria building, goal setting, or peer and self-assessment activities. I continued to attend more SALT professional training sessions, enjoying hot lunches, coffee, and cookies, and leaving with a full stomach—and mind.

Anne Davies knew my name! I was not some anonymous teacher tucked away in a small, dusty, hot classroom. Student writing seemed to be improving; classes were fun. My students and I tackled the really difficult reading assignments with enthusiasm! Plato, Camus, Marlowe! (All was right with the world!)

At the start of the 2006–07 school year, I assigned my sophomores a group project based on a summer reading assignment, William Golding's *Lord of the Flies*, a popular modern classic. I knew it would be a great way to start the year. A slam-dunk assignment. Each group was to teach some literary element of the book: characters, symbols, plot, etc. We did the deconstruction of standards, benchmarks, and performance expectations. We did criteria building. They knew all the literary terms. I even played sample student videos of successful group projects from previous years. What could go wrong? (All was well in Mudville. Full steam ahead!)

As a major piece of our Good vs. Evil unit, the novel's riveting characters and provocative questions about man's essential nature normally elicit lively discussions from students who are often in the midst of their own versions of teenage angst. Everything seemed to be falling in place, until the day of the first presentations.

The projects were boring and unimaginative: stick puppet shows, posters covered with pictures from the internet, pink pigs wearing black circular glasses, bloody pig heads with x'd out eyes, and videos with unintelligible scripts. I was in shock. What happened? It was time to regroup, to figure out what went wrong, and to take a close look at my own work. One step back. . . .

Viktor Frankl to the Rescue

Serendipity can be a great thing. At about this time, my high school senior daughter was taking the class, Ideas of Western Literature. Her assigned reading happened to be Frankl's *Man's Search for Meaning*, an account of his experience in a Nazi concentration camp and how those experiences led him to the development of logotherapy, an existential belief that man can find meaning in any set of conditions. In a death camp, this meant life. Since Frankl's book was already on my list of books to read before I die, I grabbed her copy and started reading.

Frankl observed that healthy-looking male prisoners—healthy by concentration camp standards—sometimes died for no outwardly apparent reason, while others who looked far worse were able to survive. Clearly, the will to live must've been a key, but didn't they all want to live? Of course, but at some point that instinct slowly eroded and failed to sustain life. The real questions were, What helped the inmate maintain his will to live? What factor separated the living from the dead?

The answer? Having a goal, one as simple as figuring out how to get a bit of extra bread, or how to keep that crumb for later, forced a prisoner to go on, to survive. Having a goal as seemingly insignificant as saving some food gave the prisoner something to hang on to, something that gave him hope. Creating goals gave the prisoner a sense of meaning and control over his own dismal life, much like Camus's Sisyphus contemplating his punishment and his rock, then strolling back down the hill to try again. Or, like the protagonist of Solzhenitsyn's *One Day in the Life of Ivan Denisovich*, struggling to survive in a Russian prison camp as Frankl himself did in Auschwitz. Or Ayn Rand's ideal man, Howard Roark of *The Fountainhead*, keeping his mind's eye focused on his architectural goal and, in doing so, preserving his integrity as a free-thinking man.

Is the prisoner who lacked a goal and withered away not unlike a student who does not understand what she needs to learn or where she needs to go? The less successful student might very well know what he has to do to satisfy a teacher's requirements to receive a passing score, but whose goal is that? Is he engaged? Unless he has his *own* clear picture of the learning goal or target, he may go through the motions and receive a passing grade or higher simply by turning in homework and giving the teacher rote responses, but never reach any real understanding of the material. Any lifelong learning is minimal, incidental, and happens almost by accident.

I'm sure some students whom we classify as successful, the ones regularly receiving *B*s and *A*s or enrolled in AP classes, are probably able to develop learning targets on their own, or they've figured out the system (what teachers are looking for, and what's necessary to achieve a good mark), and possibly really internalize the material to a certain degree. But what about the less successful students, many of whom are quite capable, but either haven't quite figured out the system or don't want to play? This is an issue that has often surfaced in our SALT discussions: Students become more engaged in their own learning if they believe they can succeed. However, they can't succeed if they don't understand precisely what they need to learn, and have not developed the tools that will help them become critical thinkers, a life skill. (Aaahh, relevance!)

Reflecting on my students in this way, I thought about my own school experience: I was gangbusters in elementary school and most of middle school. From around the eighth grade, much to the consternation of my mother, I became the "underachiever, who had potential." I knew I had some core intelligence, but I fell out of step with the "smart" group. I couldn't figure out what was going on. Maybe I was more interested in having fun. Or maybe it was something else. I felt out of sync, on the fringes of the "smart ones." I certainly wasn't deeply engaged in my own learning. Only my SAT scores paved the way to the university. (Oh well, at least my old high school report cards are now a source of amusement for my daughters. . . .) In any event, this pause connected me with my now underachieving students.

"Students become more engaged in their own learning if they believe they can succeed."

The dismal work produced by my students early in the 2006–07 year stemmed from a number of things. First, I was overconfident. I knew the process well enough, and I knew what the students needed to learn, but I had neglected to let them in on it. Students were willing to work and learn, but all the criteria lists and deconstruction activities were meaningless *because there was no clear learning target; they had not been fully engaged in the activity.* Second, my going through the steps by rote was satisfactory for the higher-achieving students, but not for the less successful ones who needed to learn the rules of the game. By not taking the time to clarify and to ensure that everyone was at a basic level of understanding, I unknowingly left some students in a state of confusion. Also, since no one spoke up and asked for further clarification of the assignment and what was expected, I rushed on. That was a recipe for disaster, especially at the beginning of the school year.

My perception of student involvement was not very good at that point, and when I tried to work with students once the project was well underway, it was too late. Making the wrong assumptions, skipping steps, and not checking with students resulted in a goal that was muddled so the criteria and rubrics were meaningless. Prospects of student success were greatly diminished from the very start.

I had been too product oriented and forgot to work with the students on clarifying their learning targets and the assessment process. When doing an analytical or interpretive piece of writing, I always tell students to avoid the temptation to immediately explain what something means. They have to explain to the audience what "it" says first. Good writers engage the audience and make sure an honest attempt is made to take the audience with them. I realized I had violated one of my own basic tenets: *One step at a time!* Each step should build on a previous step and prepare for the next. Skipping steps increases the likelihood that the learning process will be a bumpy road.

From deconstructing standards to creating quality lists of criteria and to practicing formative and summative assessments, students must be invited to take a more active role in their learning. The messages are clear. Student involvement is valued; everybody's important; there are many teachers in the classroom.

A Personal Story of Assessment *for* Learning

Finally, I have a story of my father who passed on a few years ago. He was a truly great teacher, an instinctively wise man and my only golf coach when I played a lot of tournaments in my younger days. I never won anything, but with him as coach and caddy, we built many unforgettable memories during practice and competition, actually, not unlike teachers and students who forge close friendships.

On the practice range, my dad always asked what I was trying to do with a particular shot or swing. . . . Hit it high? Low? Left to right? Right to left? How far? In Hawaii's broken conversational language, he'd say something like, "Look, you want ball to go one certain place, right? Feel the wind, how you want the ball to fly. Find someplace in the background like a mountain peak, tree, cloud, and send the ball that way. It'll end up in fairway or the green. Try see 'em in your head first. No get too technical. Gotta get one pictcha [picture] first. Then try." His point was that golf is a target game but you can't get too target oriented or you won't hit it.

The entire process from checking the grass to the direction and speed of the wind, even how you happen to be feeling that day . . . everything matters. There are many variables to realizing the objective, getting the ball in the cup. There was a long physical list of criteria for practice: stance, grip, weight distribution, depth of divot, sound of the swing/strike, trajectory, direction/distance, etc. There was a short list of criteria for playing: stance, setup, feel, direction/distance.

Good or bad shot, he'd often ask, "What you did on dat one? What felt like? What you goin' do on the nex' one? No just hit balls. If you wanna be good, you gotta have a purpose." He was giving immediate feedback and had me doing reflections and metacognition. He was teaching me to learn from both mistakes and successes to get closer and closer to the goal. Pretty cool, huh?

I'll never forget one incident. During one of the big local tournaments, I was walking down the twelfth fairway, not paying attention to anything in particular, and only thinking about how my final score would look on a leader board . . . and then, *thunk* . . . I kicked my own ball! PENALTY! Incredulously, he looked at me and simply asked, "What you did that for?"

"He was teaching me to learn from both mistakes and successes to get closer and closer to the goal."

Of course, I had no answer. I neglected a basic rule: know where your ball is. In fixating on the final score and prematurely congratulating myself on the twelfth hole with six more to play, I had lost sight of the process and ended up paying a severe price. My final score is long forgotten, only that sickening sound of leather on white polymer, and that very essential question remains with me.

Sometimes, when I hit the inevitable bad one, he'd say, "That's okay . . . you can still recover." His point: I can still make a good score even if I messed up the first shot, even the second, or third. There are lots of ways to make par, even birdie. It doesn't always have to be fairways and greens in regulation. At some point, though, you have to face the music and write down the final score. The more practice and formative assessment I experienced, the greater the chance for success when that summative score would be posted for all to see.

"What you did that for?" was saved for special occasions.

In the End . . . Assessment *for* Learning Works

I've come to understand that many of us have already been blessed with a skilled practitioner of assessment *for* learning as I was with my father. His voice sometimes echoes in my mind as I work with my own students to strengthen *their* learning and the quality of their current "game."

My father helped me create an image of a clear target (an understanding of what quality work looks and feels like). My mental picture of the criteria necessary for success became clearer as he pushed my thinking. He provided timely and ongoing feedback and fair formative assessment (ensuring that I understood that purposeful practice was necessary and that learning can be enhanced by recognizing mistakes and failures that clarify the necessary next steps). He also provided fair summative assessment, while reminding me that I can take what I've learned from each experience to the next challenge.

In the end, my father's lessons, a professional development that really worked, and the time and encouragement to use assessment *for* learning on my own have changed how I work each day, not only in the classroom but in everyday life.

References

Hawaii State Department of Education. (2005). Hawaii content & performance standards III database. http://165.248.30.40/hcpsv3/search_results.jsp?contentarea=Language+Arts&gradecourse=11&strand=&showbenchmark=benchmark&showspa=spa&showrubric=rubric&Go!=Submit

Acknowledgments

My sincerest thanks to mentor and friend Dr. Anne Davies, Monica Mann, retired principal Dennis Hokama, my editor Kathy, Mike Among, my father, Takeo "Shangy" Inouye, and Kelsey, my daughter who helped me overcome some technical difficulties. And also Marian's Catering!

Melissa Noack

Melissa J. Noack, B.F.A., is currently an art teacher and learning area leader for visual and performing arts at Yarmouth High School in Yarmouth, Maine. She has been teaching art for the past ten years and is working toward her master's degree in education. Melissa has presented at national and state conferences on a variety of educational topics. She was a recipient of the Sallie Mae First Class Teacher Award, National Semiconductor Internet Innovator Award, and, most recently, the Milken Educator Award. Melissa enjoys networking with other educators from around the country to continuously improve her teaching and student learning.

Action Research and the Power of Peer Feedback

by Melissa J. Noack

As a high school visual arts teacher, I am a learner. One of the most galvanizing aspects of my profession is that I am encouraged to learn—daily, weekly, forever. This learning is acquired from a variety of sources: research, ongoing course work, professional development, and especially my students. It is inherently important for me to continue to improve my own teaching and learning so that my students will have the best possible educational experience. Ultimately, my goal as a teacher is to motivate students intrinsically: to engage them deeply in the process of learning so they desire and thirst to learn. The work described in this chapter only begins to scrape the tip of the iceberg.

Foundations for Success

Throughout the 2003–04 and 2004–05 school years, the students and I built a partnership in the learning process. They knew from the beginning that, together, we were piloting a new process for critiquing artwork called *peer feedback*. The students knew they were integral players in the process and were the key to its success. The students also understood from the beginning that this was a work in progress and through their thoughtful feedback and debriefings, we would continue to improve this process until it was successful for the group as a whole.

It is essential, at the beginning of the year, to set the tone for the classroom and to make sure the expectations for students are clear. The environment in my classroom is one that encourages students to be safe, respected, and appreciated. It is also a culture that encourages risk taking, especially in regard to creative problem solving. It should be noted that I always teach heterogeneously grouped

students—students with mixed abilities, experiences, and grade levels. The action research process described here took place in an introductory art course called Foundations in Art. It involved two classes of twenty students each year. Some students entered the classroom with a strong artistic ability and lots of experience, while others may not have drawn anything since eighth grade. All students, however, are expected to show improvement throughout the year and especially from the midpoint critique to the final work of art. As a result of peer feedback, all students experienced growth and improvement over time (see Figures 6 to 10, pages 97–99). The classroom culture was vital to the success of the process.

"The motivation for students developed from within; they wanted to present their best work to each other visually and orally."

The Action Research Process

In the developmental stages of this process, I stressed the importance of students relying on each other for feedback to improve their work; I never talked about how or if I was grading the peer feedback sessions. Students were focused on the concept of developing and refining their work. The motivation for students developed from within; they wanted to present their best work to each other visually and orally. They did this through rich, meaningful dialogues guided by the use of a protocol (see Figure 1) while using arts knowledge and vocabulary.

Figure 1 ▼

Student Interview Protocol
Metamorphosis Critique

Purpose:

To engage all students in giving and receiving feedback; to hear all students' voices through small group work

Steps:

1. All students will fill out a written assessment before beginning the critique.

2. Teacher will identify four students who will interview thre students. Teacher chooses the groups.

3. Teacher will review the purpose of the unit and review the protocol.

4. The four student interviewers begin, in small groups, and interview and record the answers to the three questions (see interviewers' questions below).

5. Upon completing the interviews, the interviewers gather in the middle of the room (fishbowl style) and report their answers to the rest of the class.

6. The interviewees listen carefully to the answers of each question and record common themes to each question.

7. The process is then debriefed, informally, as a large group.

Interviewers Questions:

While listening to the answers to the questions, what are the common themes you heard in response to the questions?

1. In what ways did the midpoint critique/feedback help you to produce high-quality work?

2. If you did this project again, what would you add, change, or do differently?

3. List three important things that you learned about color from this unit or from working with a guest artist.

Adapted from Fishbowl Seminar, Protocols for Professional Learning Conversations, by Catherine Glaude, with permission.

The focus for the first year was to develop various strategies and formats for grouping students and to engage all students in prolific, eloquent dialogues. In addition, I was practicing various learning strategies that I had acquired through taking a differentiated learning course. For example, I paid close attention to and recorded observations about where students were, according to their experience and readiness level. I grouped students by mixing readiness levels so that they would receive a variety of perspectives on their work.

One of the standards in the Maine State Learning Results is to teach students how to discuss, analyze, and interpret their own work and the work of others, in order to develop a critical and informed artistic eye. In previous years, student critiques had not been successful, so using that data, I looked for a better way to achieve this goal.

The action research question I started with was: How does peer feedback help to improve student work? I began the process by organizing students into small groups to critique each other's artwork. They became much more engaged in the class through dialoguing about their work, and they enjoyed the meaningful conversations using arts knowledge and vocabulary. I knew this was a good beginning, but I wanted to take this concept to the next level where students would be held accountable for the feedback they gave or received.

The following quotes are students' thoughtful perspectives regarding their own learning as a result of participating in peer feedback sessions:

"Critiques gave me an idea what I needed to improve and how I could approach my next project differently." —B.O.C.

"I think that the critiques helped me grow as an artist because I was able to learn from my mistakes in the midpoints and how to improve to finish the final piece and make it perfect." —A.S.

"Critiques were the most meaningful/beneficial to my overall personal growth. By getting another person's perspective, I could change my pieces and learn from my mistakes." —S.G.

"Critiques gave me insight on others' thoughts compared to my own. After critiques I could change the troubled areas." —R.A.

"The critiques helped a lot in a way that I gained different techniques from others and I got different opinions from others about my work. I feel that I am a better drawer because of it!" —J.C.

"I found the critiques the most helpful because I'd never really had them before. Usually I'm the only one who sees my work and this was a pleasant change. It really helped me to look at my art from an objective point of view and learn how to improve." —A.S.

The Power of Peer Feedback

In the second year, the work moved to a different level. In addition to being engaged in rich dialogues about each other's work, students were asked to show evidence of peer feedback in their own work. They were to record the feedback from their peers and to demonstrate and explain how it helped them improve their work and learning. The results, data, and evidence that I collected surrounding this process over two years were phenomenal; it was unbelievably energizing to see the increase in student achievement across the board on so many levels. The student work and testimonials provided clear evidence that this process was successful. For the most part, students have the desire to do their best work when they are motivated by their peers. With this process, the students are less dependent on me and are using each other for feedback and as valuable resources.

The following year, I continued this process but focused specifically on the feedback. Furthermore, I wanted students to document, use, and incorporate the feedback that they received during the midpoint critique; the students' work would be the evidence. The expectation was that through the participation in peer feedback sessions, the quality and creativity of the final product would increase, as well as the students' knowledge of essential learning.

I soon learned that the process worked exceptionally well for a number of reasons. Students were relying on each other to give sound and meaningful feedback, which they documented during the midpoint critique and referred back to during their final critique. At that point, the students explained how they had used the feedback, referring to their work as evidence. They also discussed whether the feedback had made a difference in their final product, whether it was useful, and if so, how it had made a positive impact on their learning and understanding of the concepts.

Student-Directed Protocols

Another important aspect that contributed to the success of this process was the use of student-directed protocols. Having established a safe and open classroom culture where the climate and expectations were understood, it was a much easier task teaching students how to give and receive constructive criticism about their work. Because students knew and were very familiar with the criteria of the assignment, and because they had self-assessed their learning through the use of rubrics and answering reflective questions about their work, they could succeed at following a protocol and having rich, meaningful conversations.

Figures 2 and 3 are examples of protocols that I used and refined based on feedback from students during the first year. It shows my improvement in revising the first protocol to help students feel more successful. When they first began to use protocols, students indicated their need for more structure and support. In particular, their suggestion was to include prompts and ideas for what to say. This was a fabulous addition that greatly improved this tool. During the following school year, I continued to develop and revise the protocols, creating a variety of them. Figures 4 and 5 (page 96) are examples of later protocols.

Students have been an integral part of the development of the different protocols. I ask them to give me feedback by discussing whether the process was helpful and meaningful for them and if not, what change could make it more effective. I collected their data in many ways: through written self-assessments and reflections, debriefing as a group and individually, and through my observations of the small groups. Students know that I truly value their feedback; they can see their results in the next protocol that they use.

Currently, I continue the process of developing strong and meaningful protocols for students; the purpose is to support them in making better quality and creative work, while increasing student understanding of the *essential knowledge*. (This refers to the overarching skills/concepts identified by each content area, based on the state's standards, by which students are graded.)

Figures 4 and 5 (page 96)

Figure 2 ▼

Foundations in Art
Requesting Feedback Protocol

The purpose of a protocol is to develop ground rules for your group to help focus or guide your discussion. It also evens the "playing field" among the members of your group; you will all have a chance to share and discuss your ideas.

The purpose of this protocol is to **request feedback** on a specific technique or skill.

ALL STUDENTS MUST PREPARE AHEAD OF TIME. ALL STUDENTS WILL PRESENT. Decide in what area you would like feedback. This may be an area in which you have struggled or an area you may need to improve. This helps to focus the groups' attention and feedback.

Getting Started. Choose someone in your group to be a timekeeper and to keep the group on task.

Present to Group. The presenter describes what he/she set out to accomplish. Explain the criteria of the assignment. Describe what particular part of the assignment was challenging or difficult for you. (This challenge area will direct your groups' feedback.) All group members must remain silent during this presentation.

Questions. Group members ask clarifying questions about the presentation.

Reflection Time. All members of the group organize their feedback. Write notes as necessary.

Feedback. The group members brainstorm ideas and offer feedback RELATED to the challenge area. *It is important to offer constructive criticism.* The presenter remains quiet. He/she listens for any "nuggets" of information that may be helpful.

Conversation. The presenter invites the participants into a conversation to explore any of the feedback or ideas offered.

Debrief. Do a whip. How did this protocol work? How might we improve this for the future? Choose one member of your group to record this feedback and pass it in.

Adapted from Focused Feedback, *Protocols for Professional Learning Conversations,* by Catherine Glaude, with permission.

Figure 3 ▼

Foundations in Art
Receiving Feedback Protocol

The purpose of this protocol is to **offer constructive criticism to peers,** in regards to meeting the criteria of the assignment.

Please fill out the self-assessment ahead of time and review the rubric.

Step 1: (1 min) **Getting Started.** Choose someone in your group to be a timekeeper and to keep the group on task.

Step 2: (2 min) **Criteria of the Assignment.** The teacher will review the purpose and criteria of the assignment to the whole class.

Step 3: (5 min) **Present to Group.** The presenter explains how the criteria of the assignment was met, in regards to creative problem solving skills and technical skills, referring to the rubric. All group members must remain silent during this presentation. Group members may take notes or formulate questions during the presentation.

Step 4: (5 min) **Feedback/Discussion.** The group begins the discussion by asking questions to the presenter. One by one, each student asks a question to the presenter. The following is a list of questions to prompt your discussion. This will engage group members in a discussion. Please make sure everyone has time to ask at least one question.

Were you successful in communicating the idea creating a three-dimensional space? Is your perspective convincing? What strategies did you use to capture a 3-D space on a 2-D surface?
What makes your composition strong and interesting? Did you use the space well?
How well does your choice of colors work? Can you tell the difference between forms by the use of different values? Explain...
What mood is expressed by your color scheme?
Where do you fall on the rubric for creative problem-solving skills? Technical skills?
Did you enjoy this assignment? Why or why not?
Do you feel you were successful in meeting the criteria of the assignment? Why or why not?
What were your challenges or difficulties with this assignment? How did you deal with these problems? What did you learn from this?
What would you do differently next time?
How will this assignment help your future assignments?

After all students have presented, write a short debrief in the space below. Choose a person to record the following:

Step 5: (3 min) **Learnings.** Do a whip. Everyone in the group has the opportunity to speak by saying what he/she learned from this practice OR what he/she is thinking of pursuing OR questions that were raised for him/her.

Step 6: (5 min) **Debrief.** We have modified this protocol throughout the year. Do you now feel comfortable with this process of talking about your work and giving and receiving feedback? Is there anything else we could add or change? As a group (please include a comment from each person), write short paragraph and pass it in.

Adapted from Focused Feedback, *Protocols for Professional Learning Conversations,* by Catherine Glaude, with permission.

Figure 4 ▼

Midpoint Critique Feedback
Realistic Self-Portraits

Student Observation Protocol Purpose:
To give and receive feedback about the progress of your self-portrait, before using charcoal.

1. Teacher will organize students in groups according to readiness.

2. Students will decide in what order they will present and who will be the facilitator.

3. The presenting student holds up their midpoint drawing next to his/her face. The group members are silent and stare at the sketch and the person for a solid minute.

4. Each group member records areas that need improvement as well as noting what the artist has done well.

5. One by one, each group member shares their feedback with the presenting artist. The presenting artist remains quiet and records the feedback.

6. After each group member has shared his/her feedback, the presenting artist asks for any clarifying questions or prompts questions to the group for additional feedback.

7. The above steps are repeated until each group member has presented.

8. The process will be debriefed orally, after all students have presented.

9. The teacher will photograph each student's sketch.

10. The teacher will print each student's sketch. The photograph of the sketch and the written feedback will be kept in each student's portfolio; both will become part of the final portfolio for the unit.

Adapted from Focused Feedback, *Protocols for Professional Learning Conversations*, by Catherine Glaude, with permission.

Figure 5 ▼

Foundations in Art—Drawing Unit
Final Critique Protocol

Purpose: To share your learning, techniques, and skills with other students; to expand the interpretation of your work by encouraging different viewpoints and voices of others

ALL STUDENTS WILL PRESENT.
Students will fill out the self-assessment ahead of time. Teacher will group students into clusters of three or four students per table.

1. (2 min) **Criteria of the Assignment.** The teacher will review the protocol, the purpose, and criteria of the assignment to the whole class.

2. (1 min) **Getting Started.** Choose someone in your group to be a timekeeper and to keep the group on task. Decide in what order each member will present.

3. (5 min) **Present to Group.** The presenter describes how the feedback from the midpoint critique affected his/her final drawing. The presenter should show evidence by referring to the drawing. In addition, the presenter describes a piece of learning, technique, or skill that was meaningful and significant (this may be a successful aspect of the drawing; you may also refer to your portfolio of progress). All group members must remain silent during this presentation.
   Listening. As the presenter is speaking, each member of the group listens for and records one piece of evidence that shows the presenter understands and/or can demonstrate the essential learning of the assignment; or how the presenter has shown growth since the beginning of the year.

4. (2 min) **Feedback.** Each member, one by one, reads aloud the documentation of evidence of learning or progress from his/her note card.

5. (2 min) **Final Word.** All group members hand their feedback to the presenter. The presenter reviews the feedback silently and chooses one that significantly stands out. The presenter reads it aloud to the group.

6. **Repeat steps 3, 4, and 5** until all members of the group have presented.

After all students have presented, write a short debrief in the space below. The facilitator records the following on a piece of paper to give the teacher. Include all names of group members.

7. (3 min) **Learnings.** What did you learn as a result of this unit of study? The facilitator records each group member's thoughts.

8. (3 min) **Debrief the Process.** What worked well for you? What could we do differently next time to improve this process?

Adapted from Learning from Success Stories, *Protocols for Professional Learning Conversations*, by Catherine Glaude, with permission.

Evidence of Success

Student work is evidence that this strategy is working. All students, even with differing experiences and ability levels, have achieved success by the end of each unit (see Figures 6 and 7). Through using sound protocols and engaging in rich, meaningful dialogues during midpoint critiques, students are able to reach this goal. Moreover, by encouraging students to rely on each other for feedback, they are becoming more self-directed and better problem solvers. I have witnessed evidence of this through observing students and their work in the classroom. As the teacher, I am no longer the first person a student asks for feedback. Students are working toward finding solutions to creative problems collaboratively, in pairs, or in small groups.

The evidence supported my theory and improved the quality and creativity of the students' work. However, there are always challenges that occur with successes. The two biggest challenges that I encountered are dealing with group dynamics and making sure the feedback that the students are receiving is accurate, helpful, and meaningful. I recently had a couple of students who felt that the feedback they received during the midpoint critique was not at all helpful. They thought the group members were just being agreeable and did not offer any specific ways to improve the work. The way I handled that was to recommend to those few students to be sure to see me for specific feedback after the midpoint critique if they did not get the feedback they felt was necessary. I continue to work on this aspect, as it is critical that all, not just select, students benefit from the peer feedback sessions.

Figure 6 ▼

Figure 7 ▼

Student engagement and motivation has increased tremendously in my classroom. Because students understand that their work will be viewed and constructively critiqued by their peers, not just by me, they are more motivated to do quality work. Because students are engaged and care about learning how to improve their work, I have experienced fewer classroom management and behavior problems; they practically ceased to exist. The entire process helps to create a collaborative learning environment that benefits all students and thus gives them a powerful learning experience! The progress and results of a sampling of student work are shown in Figures 8, 9, and 10 (pages 98–99).

"All students, even with differing experiences and ability levels, have achieved success by the end of each unit."

Student Work—Progress Over Time (Midpoint and Final Still Drawing)

Figure 8 ▼

Figure 9 ▼

 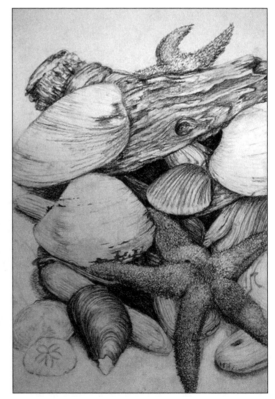

"Grades were never a motivational factor."

Conclusion

This has been an inspirational and highly beneficial process both for the students and for me. It is a process that engages students and encourages them to demonstrate higher-level thinking skills without being formally evaluated or graded. Grades were never a motivational factor.

I learned that peer feedback sessions would not be quite so successful had they not been conducted through the use of protocols. With the students giving me feedback along the way, I developed many different protocols for them to use to structure their conversations. In addition to the use of protocols, the climate and culture in the classroom led to the huge success of this action research.

This type of research is a powerful and effective teaching tool, in that changes can be made immediately as the data are collected and reflected upon. This makes action research more meaningful and more likely to impact student learning.

Every year, the process continues to evolve and be refined. I now have documented evidence of success that I share with each new class; this becomes the building block for the current group of students. In conclusion, I will continue to revise, change, and reflect on my practice so that I am constantly improving my teaching and student learning. Collaborative work is a positive and galvanizing experience for everyone!

References

Coalition for Essential Schools. Box 1969, Brown University, Providence, RI 02912. *www.essentialschools.org*

Davies, A. (2011). *Making classroom assessment work* (3rd ed.). Bloomington, IN: Solution Tree Press.

Glaude, C. (2005). *Protocols for professional learning conversations: Cultivating the art and discipline.* Courtenay, BC: Connections Publishing.

McDonald, J. P., Mohr, N., Dichter, A., and McDonald, E. C. (2003). *The power of protocols: An educator's guide to better practice.* New York: Teachers College Press.

Sagor, R. (1992). *How to conduct collaborative research.* Alexandria, VA: Association for Supervision and Curriculum Development.

Tomlinson, C. A. (1999). *The differentiated classroom: Responding to the needs of all learners.* Alexandria, VA: Association for Supervision and Curriculum Development.

Note: The protocols used with students, examples of student work, and student testimonials can be viewed at *https://sites.google.com/a/yarmouthschools.org/melissa -noack/*

Murray Guest

Murray Guest has been a classroom teacher for twenty years in Saskatchewan. He has a degree in physics and did his masters work on the educational gains that can be made by removing grades from educational settings. He teaches physics and mathematics, including AP calculus and IB standard-level mathematics. He also designs programs to help students who struggle with math. Murray has years of training in creativity studies and, before he started teaching in high schools, spent time training people in methods to promote creative solutions to problems.

Mathematics Teachers Are Ahead of the Curve When It Comes to Assessment *for* Learning

by Murray Guest

As the phrase "assessment *for* learning" is used more and more, some mathematics teachers find themselves wondering how their practice conforms to its precepts. They wonder whether they are behind the times. In some people's minds, assessment *for* learning seems to be better suited to the humanities or perhaps even the sciences, but it doesn't fit well with mathematics. I think mathematics teachers are in a great position with regard to assessment *for* student learning. I am confident that math teachers have many teaching practices that follow assessment *for* learning recommendations and lead to student improvement. And yet, we, like all teachers, are challenged to continue to learn and change. This chapter proposes that math teachers have been leaders, in some cases without knowing it, in the use of assessment *for* learning.

Research-Based Practices

Assessment *for* learning (AFL) involves using assessment in the classroom to increase learning and raise pupils' achievement. AFL is based on the idea that students will improve most if they understand the goals of their learning, where they are in relation to those goals, and how they can close the gap between where they are and where they need to be. This approach to education is based on decades of research from many sources. The results of this research are not in dispute.

Assessment *for* learning is a research-based theory of learning and teaching that has many components, all of which have been shown to improve student learning. Key ideas include:

- Providing clear learning targets
- Using samples and exemplars of student work to help students understand quality
- Providing continuous, high-quality feedback from a variety of sources

The recommendations regarding assessment *for* learning based on the research also emphasize the importance of multiple opportunities for students to revise their work based on the feedback they receive, as well as the provision for students to provide alternative proof of what they have learned.

*"Math teachers have been leaders, in some cases without knowing it, in the use of assessment **for** learning."*

It is anticipated that teachers using AFL will engage in formative assessment; that is, they will use the information gathered from student assessment to alter their teaching based on student strengths and address needs identified from the assessment process. The "assessment" part of assessment *for* learning refers to the gathering of information regarding student understanding, knowledge of application, and articulation of mathematical ideas. Teachers then use that information to support both student learning and teacher practice. Evaluation comes after assessment *for* learning and is most accurate when it is based on most recent, most consistent evidence of learning rather than grades of all assessments taken during the school year. This is a key point for many mathematics teachers. Rather than averaging or using some other mathematical formula to determine the final grade, teachers look at the evidence of learning collected and determine whether it is useful in providing an accurate account of what has been learned in relation to the course outcomes.

Transforming Current Practices

Assessment can be formal or informal. Formal assessments include tests, writing samples, or student projects. Less formal sources of assessment information include observations of a student working, conversations regarding the current assignment, or a one-question quiz at the end of the class to check students' understanding of the day's work. There are many practices in mathematics classes that illustrate assessment *for* learning in action. For example:

- Assignments with an available answer key allow students to self-assess their knowledge to obtain continuous feedback.

- When teachers of mathematics walk around checking work and talking with students, they are providing feedback as well as gathering and regarding student understanding of mathematical concepts.

- Handing back a piece of student work with corrections and written ideas for improvements can also offer students high-quality feedback.

These types of assessment *for* learning have been done for years in mathematics classes; however, it is important to take these actions with explicit intent and to ensure that students understand why we are doing these things.

Students must be aware of the reasons for having this feedback and of how to use this feedback to help their learning. Those students we would traditionally consider good students are often able to do this on their own without much prompting by the teacher. Struggling students are often unable to translate teacher feedback into better performance.

Like many teachers, I give regular quizzes in my class. One change I made in my practice is to make explicit to students that the point of the quizzes is to have the students check to see what they know and what they don't know regarding an area of study. To increase the likelihood that this is the only message students are given regarding quizzes, I offer no grades for the quizzes. I explain to students why I don't grade practice. The only change I needed to make to conform to AFL was to remove the grades on quizzes and other practice work.

"Homework is ... practice and should not be graded."

Homework is practice. The point of doing homework is to gain automaticity with the material and to identify problems in students' understanding of material. It is still practice and should not be graded. I justify this by asking how often I was graded, based on a practice drive as I learned to handle a car or if I was judged as I refined my skills on the volleyball court. Once students understand the reasons for the assigned practice and see that it works, they do it without complaint. Those who don't do it will learn of its value through trial and error. I still check homework so I can identify problems with students' understanding, but that checking reinforces the message I want to send regarding homework. If a student chooses to not do homework and yet needs to have that practice, I talk with them and provide closer supervision. Students come to understand that homework is useful in our goal of understanding math better, rather than something to gather grades (or to punish or reward them). It helps students see me as someone who is there to support their learning.

Being clear with students about what they need to learn, I give them a list of standards for each unit. Then I have students go through it with me, thinking about their own work. They are expected to write about what they do well, what they struggle with, and why they believe that is the case. This process supports student understanding of where they are with respect to math standards as well as meeting some of the requirements regarding communicating mathematically. The process is collaborative, student centered, and by my students' own admission, useful. This account of their learning is saved and used later as students reflect on and collect evidence of their learning in relation to the mathematics standards.

Math teachers have always tried to be responsive to student needs. When we look at the results of a midunit quiz, or know, through teacher-student interaction, that a large portion of the class may not understand a concept, then we spend more time with it and reteach concepts. We spend individual time with certain students who we see, through informal assessment, may need extra help to understand a concept. Math teachers already explain a concept in many different ways using visual aids, manipulatives, and real-world examples. When a student asks a math teacher for help, that is a self-assessment. Our response is collaboration with the student to help them understand the mathematical concept with which they are struggling. The change? We now explain to students what mathematics teachers do to support their learning, how we think it helps, and invite students to identify other things we could do to support their learning.

"By being explicit about my expectations, students better understood the purpose of each task and activity."

Only recently I've begun writing clearly on the board what I hope the students will understand, be able to do, and be able to articulate by the end of class. An example would be: "Today you will be able to find the reference angle for any given angle, and you will find the exact value of a trig function using reference angles." This allows students to know exactly what is expected of them from the beginning of the class. I was surprised that many of my students did not know what I wanted them to know at the end of the class. By being explicit about my expectations, students better understood the purpose of each task and activity. Making explicit all of the learning targets for each class and keeping to that learning target has been a powerful change, although there are still times when I want my students to get to the targets on their own. In this case, I will use the learning targets at the end of class rather than the beginning.

A final area of change involves evidence of learning, which can take many forms. The traditional form for math teachers is the unit test and comprehensive final. They offer students a chance to show what they know by working a set of problems in a set amount of time. Alternatives do exist. Some examples: Students can write regarding their understanding of various mathematical techniques—explaining how and why specific techniques work, with a discussion of their strengths and weaknesses. Students can also devise or strengthen existing questions, with an accompanying explanation of why the work done reflects an understanding of concepts. They can work through real-world questions, either alone or in a group, grappling with the messy nature of problems that are not "cooked" for the classroom. Although they are considered time consuming, student interviews can give a very good picture of what students understand and don't have to be awkward. They can be short and focus on a single concept. For example, I like to talk to my students individually regarding the expansion of a squared binomial like $(x - 3)^2$. The reason for this is that many students choose to use their own rule to "distribute the square" and end up with either $(x - 3)^2 = x^2 - 9$ or $(x - 3)^2 = x^2 + 9$. I might follow up on their answers by asking them about the statement $(5 - 3)^2 = 5^2 - 3^2 = 16$ as a parallel example or ask them to compare the factored form of $x^2 - 9$ to $(x - 3)^2$ and explain where they see differences. If they answer my initial question with $(x - 3)^2 = x^2 - 6x + 9$, I might ask why it isn't $x^2 + 9$ or ask them to explain their work in English rather than the language of mathematics. By tailoring the follow-up questions to allow students to explain their thinking and struggle with inconsistencies, I get a better insight into their thoughts and the students get a chance to rearrange their own understanding of math concepts. Math teachers have done this, both at the board in larger groups and with individuals, for years and years. The difference is that I am explicitly working to assess the misconception of the students, whatever that might be, and then engage students so that they rearrange their concepts. I can convert this into short notes to follow up on and be more confident in my insights into the quality of the understanding held by my students.

By opening the door to alternative ways of showing understanding, we as teachers can also invite our own students to devise acceptable ways of demonstrating proof of learning that we may not have thought of ourselves. By rearranging our work, we can spend more time assessing our students and responding to the understanding they show, and less time defining the form student understanding must take.

This chapter examines what I believe to be the practice of many mathematics teachers and compares that practice to the precepts of assessment *for* learning. While we still have some challenges to address, we mathematics teachers have less to apologize for than some people would suppose.

Cris Rathyen

Cristina C. Rathyen, Ph.D., attended local-language elementary and high schools in Sweden, Germany, and New Zealand, and is a strong advocate for inclusion, intellectual safety, and multicultural education. She invented and taught a specialized high school curriculum for regular education students that integrates art, music, and English, and was awarded a Christa McAuliffe Fellowship for her work in this area. She has also taught graduate-level curriculum theory as adjunct faculty at the University of Hawaii, and was the AP English, Humanities/English, and Yearbook teacher at Moanalua High School in Honolulu, Hawaii, for twenty-two years. Additionally, she is a National Board Certified English teacher and was a featured columnist for the *Honolulu Star Bulletin*, a consultant for the College Board Advanced Placement English program, and, having recently retired, is presently engaged in reinventing herself.

Engaging Students in Self-Assessment Through Letter Writing

by Cris Rathyen

I teach a writing-intensive line that usually includes two sections of Advanced Placement English literature (average 55 students), two sections of a senior English course called Humanities/English (average 50 students), and the yearbook (which this year was 320 pages of full color). In order to balance the paperwork load generated by these various programs, I use different grading and reading strategies for my different classes. One of those strategies is to engage my Humanities/English sections in letter writing and portfolio grading. The Humanities/English class is a specialized curriculum I designed to facilitate students in interactions with a variety of different kinds of text. Instead of stories and poems, students usually work with images and music as sources and are asked to respond to those alternate texts in a variety of ways, including analysis, creative writing, and personal reflection. This class is composed of students of all ability levels, from the profoundly challenged to high-ability students searching for alternatives to the traditional English focus on linguistic analysis and formal writing instruction.

In order to differentiate instruction and assessment in the Humanities/English classes and to accommodate diverse learning needs of my students, I use writing portfolios for assessment but I have expanded the traditional portfolio system by including an ongoing personal letter exchange. This is designed to personalize learning and to engage students in self-assessment. Although exchanging personal letters with my students on a one-to-one basis every three weeks does take a lot of time, the trade-off for me is that students self-select their best work for formal/summative assessment and I read their work holistically, rather than marking individual papers.

I work with my students individually as their writing is in process, helping them with drafting and organization, so that when the writing portfolios land on my desk, most of the pieces are already familiar to me. Then I can evaluate the strongest and weakest aspects of the writing and respond to that in a personal letter to each student. In this way, I avoid the day-to-day grind of marking hundreds of papers for minor mistakes. My students learn that they need to draft their work, think about their writing, and ask for help in getting their best pieces ready for summative assessment. They get feedback during the writing process in terms of how to improve their work, but this feedback is informal and ongoing, on an as-needed basis. The portfolios, on the other hand, are all turned in at the same time and assessed at the same time. I have to plan for "portfolio weeks" so that during those weeks I do not have a major yearbook deadline or a set of formal papers due from the AP students. With some careful planning, I take a whole week to read, evaluate, and write, and I return all portfolios to my students on the same day.

"I avoid the day-to-day grind of marking hundreds of papers for minor mistakes."

The early letters set the tone for what I expect, as well as establish personal relationships between me and my students. At first they focus more on content than performance, and as my students find their voices as writers, later letters offer more constructive suggestions and criticisms to help them improve.

The letter exchange between my students and me serves to:
- Establish intellectual safety in the classroom
- Forge personal relationships between teacher and student
- Differentiate both instruction and assessment
- Encourage engagement through self-assessment

How the Letter-Writing Process Works

Every three weeks or so, students select their best writing pieces and then correspond with me about their selections, their learning, and, if they wish, their own lives. Their letters are placed with the best work selections into the portfolios along with all the other day-to-day assignments, and are given to me for consideration. I reply individually to each student, addressing first the personal issues that are in their letters, then the content of the writing, and last, the performance level of the pieces (both the best work and the assignments as a whole). My letters average between one and two pages, double spaced and typed. All letters are returned to the class during the same period. Although this takes a lot of time, I don't do any other take-home grading for my Humanities/English classes and time my letters around my other commitments.

When I return the portfolio with my letter in it, I also assign a suggested grade for the portfolio as a whole and provide specific guidance to students on how to improve their work. Grades are based on the best and/or most recent work, and the final grade for the course is a reflection of student achievement in writing and reading at the end of the year.

The letters I exchange with my students evolve over the school year. Initially, I focus on the interactions with my students, rather than on evaluative assessment, in order to forge relationships of trust. By focusing first on the student, and secondarily on formal assessment, I shift the responsibility for that assessment from teacher to learner. In other words, what I ask my students to do is to evaluate and interact with their own work and then to share that evaluation with me in a letter. This encourages self-assessment through metacognition and requires students to identify and work toward achieving their individual learning goals. However, even though students can be very accurate in their self-assessment, it was difficult for me at first to let go of the traditional stance of "evaluate and grade" in preference to a more humanistic goal of "relate and guide." *Nevertheless, I have discovered that when I focus on learning rather than on summative assessment, the students also focus on learning.* The result is that assessment becomes a tool for learning. Furthermore, once students realize that there is an active reader of their writing who is listening to their ideas and who is searching for evidence of *what they do well*, the quality of that writing improves and students become engaged and motivated.

"By taking ownership in their own learning, students engage deeply in the process."

In their letters to me, students are able to contextualize their writing. In fact, they create their own grading context—in other words, the letter exchange allows students to explain and articulate their interaction with their own work. This empowers my students and the letter exchange becomes a highly prized event. Often the letters that struggling students, write are the best developed and longest pieces of writing that they produce. I believe this is because the letters are an opportunity for communication, reflection, and personalization—and by taking ownership in their own learning, students engage deeply in the process. As one student put it recently:

"The assignment that I like working on every quarter is writing these letters to you telling you about how we're doing, not many teachers care about that but you do. . . . I also like these letters because we can be honest and tell you if we're having trouble in a certain area in class."

The letter exchange creates an environment where the emphasis is on personal learning, rather than competitive grading. This mitigates the fear of failure that seems to be a part of the writing process for many students, and the conversation between me and my students becomes one where learning, assessment, and reflection are integrated as an organic whole.

To illustrate how letter writing works, the following example letter is annotated to show the various components:

Dear Suzy,

Thank you for your long and chatty letter. I'm sorry that you are having a tough time balancing your job and school, but I can see that because of the sacrifices you are making in giving up your recreational time, you are getting all of your class work done. Good for you! I worked all through my senior year at the university at a really horrible job, seven days a week, and oddly it's the job that I remember best about that year. I guess hard times really forge memories! **[Respond to the student personally and make some kind of connection with his or her personal life.]**

I enjoyed reading your portfolio. I laughed out loud at your version of "Girl" by Jamaica Kinkaid, and I could just hear your mother nagging you. Nagging is a form of love, but sometimes it can be, as you clearly show, annoying. However, I did agree with you, as amusing as your "Girl" rewrite is, the personal essay piece is your best work. This essay is organized, has a strong central focus on your job, and gives a real-life glimpse into who you are and why the university should admit you. **[Let the student know you are an active reader of all of the work and recognize his or her efforts at self-assessment. If the student makes a mistake in identifying which piece is the best work, gently point out why another piece has stronger attributes, and make that guidance very clear.]**

Your writing is carefully edited and proofread, but I think you should work on expanding your ideas. Nearly every piece in the portfolio left me wishing that there was more there—in other words, you are excellent at creating a world and bringing your reader into it, but you don't develop that world fully enough. It isn't so much about length, as it is about experiences—try to include more experiences, and more stories, in your narrative pieces. *[Identify what the student is doing well and suggest attainable and specific learning goals for the particular student for the future.]*

Finally, I'm troubled by the fact that you didn't include any analytical pieces in your selections, even though slide analysis was one of the things I listed for this portfolio check. Analytical writing is one of the English standards, and you will need to demonstrate your ability to write analytically before the end of the year. Please be sure to include at least one analytical piece of writing—slide or story analysis—the next time. *[Identify deficits that need to be made up so the student can meet all course goals.]*

Again, thanks so much for your lovely letter, and I really enjoyed reading your insights on the class as a whole. I'm glad that you like the class, and I appreciate your grumbling about the increasing difficulty of the assignments. Since you are doing those assignments well, I don't see this as a problem, but if you ever feel that you cannot do what is being asked, please let me know and I'll "lighten up." *[Show student that he or she is empowered to request and expect changes in the learning environment and that you value the input.]*

Your portfolio grade is a B plus. Clearly, you could be earning an A by just being a little more thorough in your work. You meet the basic standards, but you haven't exceeded all of them, and I'm still waiting for the analytical writing. *[Student knows exactly where he or she is in terms of evaluative assessment, but that assessment is a suggestion rather than a hurdle that must be overcome.]*

Love,
Rath
[Letter concludes with an informal salutation to reinforce the friendly nature of the exchange.]

PS: don't forget that your YaYa Box project is coming up in two weeks, so you should probably get started on that. Ask me if you have any questions about how to make the box. *[Remind the student about upcoming projects.]*

This letter is very typical of my letter exchanges with students. It takes time to think about all the components that must be included when writing the first set of letters, but once personal learning relationships are established with students, they become responsible to direct attention to the standards and learning goals demonstrated in their work. They do the searching and evaluation, not I. By personalizing my interactions with my students from the beginning of the year, the day-to-day focus in my classroom shifts from an ongoing effort to read and respond to every single paper, to a holistic response to each learner as a human being who has identified and contextualized his or her best work. The letters become a conversation between friends and thus are enjoyable for me and for my students.

"The letters become a conversation between friends."

Each letter includes the following components:

- A personal response to the student, making connections between my own life and the concerns of the student
- Responses to any issues that are expressed by the student regarding assignments or the learning environment
- Praise for what the student did well
- A comment on the student-selected best work; this is an affirmation of success or constructive guidance to the student regarding the accuracy of the self-assessment
- Some suggestions for improvement based on the student's needs and ability levels
- A general summative evaluation of the work in the writing portfolio as a whole and a suggestion of how a student might improve his or her summative evaluation for the next portfolio check—with a clear explanation for why a certain grade was assigned to the portfolio
- An identification of any major deficits or problem areas that could create difficulties later in the year
- Guidance and reminders about upcoming projects for weaker students
- A friendly salutation

Using Letters to Forge Relationships and Create Intellectual Safety

The first set of letters take the most time for me because those letters establish working relationships with every student. I craft these letters very carefully and write the personal response to the students before I address assessment in any way.

I try to find something in the student letter or in the student's writing portfolio that I can connect to events or interests in my own life, and I reveal aspects of my family, history, and personal feelings in my responses. The letters allow me to interact with my students personally, identify their individual perspectives and needs, and respond to those needs, whether they are academic, personal, or behavioral.

Letter writing gives a voice to the concerns of special needs and struggling students and helps create an intellectually safe environment for them. For example, one of my special needs students wrote in his first letter that he was "slow" and was worried about his ability to do well in English. He commented:

> "Many times I have problems focusing. So when I have assignments, I have to read the instructions to try to understand what I need to do."

He went on to talk about how difficult school was for him, and how he lacked the necessary skills to go to college. My response focused primarily on addressing his self-image, since it was clear from his portfolio that John had excellent literacy skills. I shared this with him:

"Letter writing gives a voice to the concerns of special needs and struggling students."

> "I remember that our son's first-grade teacher tried to tell us that Jason couldn't learn to read and write because he was slow, but what we found out the following year was that he just needed more time to process instructions, more time to think about what he was writing, and that he never did well when pushed. I see you the same way—clearly you write well, think well, and have deep and profound insights to what you see and hear. . . . Don't give up on your dreams, John, and don't think you aren't good at English, because you are!!"

I went on in the letter to outline a plan for him that included reducing the number of assignments required and setting up brief meetings to clarify all instructions. Through this initial letter exchange, I was able to identify and act on John's particular learning needs, as well as to inaugurate a friendly and supportive conversation.

When drafting the initial set of letters to my students, I consider their first letter to me, their journals, their contributions in class, and everything in their writing portfolios. I read their work the first time through, as a friend looking for a personal connection that I can articulate in my inaugural letter. I focus on the messenger, rather than on the quality of the message. In other words, I read initially for content, and I look for aspects of a student's personal life that I can chat about. Once I have initiated an informal exchange and written the personal response portion of my letter, then I read their work a second time in order to assess where they are academically. I evaluate the degree to which students are able to self-assess their work, and I try to respond to those assessments in a supportive and friendly way. The letters are a conversation about learning, providing me with insights into work habits, learning styles, and personal issues. This facilitates the differentiation of both instruction and assessment for every student in the class.

Letters help me evaluate student work as part of an organic process that begins with self-assessment and ends with personal and private communication in an environment of mutual trust. As one student commented, "Trust is what inspires me to actually do my humanities homework." The letters are so important to the students that when portfolios are returned with these letters in them, there is complete and absorbed silence in the room until all the letters are read. Often, students read their letters several times before closing their portfolios to begin the day.

"It's the personal touch that creates the magic of an intellectually safe classroom."

It's the personal touch that creates the magic of an intellectually safe classroom because intellectual safety isn't a product of a set of rules posted on the wall, but rather is fostered through the exchange of stories, personal anecdotes, and honest interactions. The letters that I exchange with my students become for us a bridge of trust and respect. The privacy and intimacy of personal correspondence is an important instructional tool in helping me identify and meet the personal learning needs of my students.

Exchanging personal letters with students requires taking some risks because I have to model for my students the same honesty that I am asking of them. For example, in a letter to me, one of my students revealed that he had moved and changed schools multiple times. It was evident from David's classroom behavior and from his letter that he felt disenfranchised from school and from his classmates. I thought that his mixed ethnic heritage, coupled with the constant moving, might have had something to do with his negative attitude, so I responded to David's first letter by noting:

> *"I was interested to read that you are also a military dependent, as I am. We moved eighteen times in twenty-four years, and boy did I get sick and tired of packing and unpacking. We retired here, too, and love it. I think you and I have a lot in common, and*

here's one more thing—my grandchild's mother is Filipina. Our granddaughter is beautiful with those big huge eyes and she's so bright and funny."

By trusting David with revelations regarding my personal history and my relationship with my grandchild, I also opened the door for him to trust me with his own thoughts and ideas. David knew from my letters to him that I was interested in him as a person and that I was reading his thoughts and ideas not only as his teacher, but also as a fellow traveler in life. Furthermore, by telling stories about my life in letters to him, I could model for a shy and withdrawn student the power of a personal and revelatory voice in writing. Later in the year, David wrote, "Your room, to me, is a sanctuary."

Granted, it can be problematic to reveal aspects of one's personal life and feelings to students, but something wonderful happens in an intellectually safe classroom where trust permeates the environment. My students know me as a person and they believe that when I assess their work, I am doing it because I care about them and their success. They have ownership in the learning environment because they participate in a respectful and private conversation with me and they are empowered to explain their difficulties and articulate their successes.

"Something wonderful happens in an intellectually safe classroom where trust permeates the environment."

Letters as a Tool for Differentiating Instruction and Assessment

Throughout the year, the emphasis in instruction and assessment is on process, rather than product. I read all the work submitted each portfolio check and respond not just to the student-selected best pieces, but also to the body of work as a whole, searching for evidence of learning. When students fail to select their best work for summative assessment, I identify the better piece and explain my reasoning. I assess their work by looking for what they do well, and my letters to them are meant to guide them toward maximizing their strengths and overcoming their weaknesses. By reading and responding to student work as part of a one-on-one conversation, the letters allow me to differentiate both instruction and assessment.

To illustrate, in responding to three students who had all selected the same assignment as a sample of their best writing, I changed my vocabulary and guidance, based on the different learning needs of those students. The assignment asked students to create a correspondence between the painter Gauguin and a mythical French society woman protesting about the nudity in Gauguin's work. To do this effectively, students had to understand the difference between a collective and an individual culture viewpoint and be able to create letters that showed the opposing points of view. In responding to a highly proficient student writer, I commented:

> *"I really liked the Gauguin letters—you clearly delineate the cultural differences, and your letters were both amusing and articulate. I think what I like best about your work is the way you change voice for different situations—you can write very well in a variety of genres and this is a strength that will definitely help you in college."*

This response addresses conceptual issues in the student work, uses high-level vocabulary, and integrates writing-specific terms such as voice and genre. I commented to all three students about what they did well, but while my response to the high-ability student was abstract, in responding to a less proficient student writer, I offered concrete suggestions for improvement:

"Personalizing instruction and assessment is a powerful tool for academic change."

> *"I loved the Gauguin letters—you got the irate tone exactly right, and you show in those letters that you can change writing style for a variety of purposes. However, and this is something I see in all your pieces with the possible exception of the lake discussion, you tend to SAY rather than SHOW. If you want to have power in your writing, you need to draw the reader into your world. The only way to do this is by detail and discussion.*
>
> *Give examples, describe events and people, draw your reader into the world that you are trying to write about. . . ."*

The two different responses tailor both assessment feedback and ongoing instruction to meet different student academic needs. Most English teachers tell their students repeatedly that in writing, they should show, not tell. By giving this guidance to a struggling student in a personal letter, I also personalized this particular writing lesson to this particular student's needs. I have found that personalizing instruction and assessment is a powerful tool for academic change.

Sometimes a letter might address an affective, rather than an academic, need. For this same Gauguin assignment, I used my response to a third student's work to "chat" because this student was working well, but seemed disengaged from the class and the curriculum. Consequently, I focused on the content of his writing to forge a connection, commenting in my letter:

"I laughed out loud at your Gauguin letters—Peter Parker!!! How funny is that!! And then you have Gauguin respond with a comment about different lifestyles—wouldn't you say that Peter Parker has a lifestyle totally NOT like anyone else? When I was a kid I used to dream of being Spider Girl—I thought the idea of flying through the air on a web was just the coolest thing going."

The informal language and tone of my response reinforces the idea of the letters as a friendly exchange that can be off topic and personal. In the three responses to the same assignment, my letters ranged from (1) providing abstract commentary for a high-achieving student who needed affirmation that she was on track for college-level writing; to (2) identifying immediate and basic writing deficits to a struggling student who required specific and finite guidance; and finally to (3) using student writing as an opener for a friendly conversation about Spider people in order to foster engagement. The power in using letters to communicate with students about their work is that you can individualize the interaction, the instruction, and the assessment.

Some of my students are working at very high levels, and I try to engage them in conversations that will give them ideas to consider beyond the assignments they present in their portfolios. For example, here is my response to a personal essay assignment to one of my high-performing students:

"Your essay brought to mind what the philosopher Aristotle said thousands of years ago about friendship. He distinguishes friendship into three kinds: utility (people who are useful to each other, like lab partners, soccer teammates, things like that); pleasure (you hang out with these guys and enjoy doing the same stuff); and perfected (the friend who is there for you no matter what). Your whole essay on this topic just reminded me so much of these distinctions and I would have to say that you have the mind and heart of a philosopher."

It isn't surprising that after this very brief lesson on philosophy, this student's next essay exhibited a focus on ideas and that he went beyond the literary analysis and discussion to make some personal connections with the text in a conceptual and philosophical way. Discussing Aristotle with a student is one end of a spectrum of responses. My letter regarding Amy's personal essay was much less abstract. In response, I wrote:

"It would help if you proofread your materials and used spell check. You want your best work to truly represent your best, and not show you as a sloppy writer."

The gentle reprimand in this letter was in part a response to Amy's comment, "I don't think that there was much of a problem with any of the assignments or the curriculum. I think that the problem was really me and my laziness." Amy was attentive in class, but she tended to procrastinate in completing her writing portfolio. Agreeing with her self-appraisal about her laziness, I both acknowledged the problem and validated her own self-awareness. Her next writing portfolio was submitted on time and the work was spell checked and proofread.

Encouraging students to live up to their own best abilities is built into the letters. By asking students to reach beyond their present levels of analysis and writing, while still acknowledging what they are doing well, the letters encourage students to take risks and to work toward higher-level thinking skills. Even when an analysis of a text shows some misreads, rather than criticizing the errors in analysis, I identify what the student did well and focus on that in my letter.

Letters offer an ideal opportunity for reteaching a lesson that only some students need to hear a second time. For example, I assigned the painting *Christina's World*, by Andrew Wyeth, as a text for analysis. Students worked first in groups to analyze the image and then wrote up their ideas in short papers. One of the learning goals of this assignment was to give students practice in making careful observations before going to the next step of analysis and explanation. In spite of specific guidance to the contrary, some students leap into analysis before taking the time to see what is actually in the text. In responding to this issue, I wrote to one student:

"Next time I would like to see you open your analysis with a general summary of what is in the image and how it is constructed, and then follow that with an in-depth discussion by category. . . ."

This student is being reinstructed to proceed through the steps of observation before analysis in an orderly and coherent fashion. To another student I wrote:

"You are a keen observer of art, and your observation and analysis of Christina's World are both wonderful. However, I would like to

see you change your style to a more narrative voice. Instead of just listing your observations and the analysis in a bullet format and then responding in a narrative to the text, next time please look on the analysis exercises as miniexpository essays. Begin with a written introduction where you outline what is physically in the work, and then go on to observations with analysis, and finally to your response, using narrative voice throughout."

The first instruction gives some general guidelines to a student who needs to understand the sequence, whereas the second instruction leads a strong student to begin using a nonlinguistic text for a narrative piece of exposition. By individualizing my response to student work and by using feedback rather than evaluation to interact with students and their writing, the letters articulate clear and achievable learning goals for each student. I am consciously using assessment *for* learning to stretch their thinking and move their work forward.

The important thing in responding to student work through a letter exchange is to listen to what students are saying, both in their writing and in their letters. As one student so beautifully put it, "I appreciate how you value our opinions and thoughts." If students believe that the teacher will read their work with the idea in mind that they have something valuable to say, they will want to articulate their opinions and thoughts to the best of their ability.

Using Letters to Encourage Engagement Through Self-Assessment

In my classroom, students have the opportunity to reflect on their work before selecting their best efforts for summative assessment. I identify what I consider important writing assignments, but students are given choices about which pieces best meet the standards in English, and which show their best work as writers. They then take those choices and edit them for summative grading.

Our school uses a standards-based grading system where formative work is assessed but not graded. Only summative assignments count for the final grade, and in a portfolio system using letters, students can select those assignments they wish to have graded. By giving my students this choice, I encourage them to become engaged in the business of achieving excellence.

Corresponding with students in a portfolio grading system gives students the opportunity to go through their work, self-assess its quality, identify their best pieces, and then contextualize those pieces for the teacher/reader. However, the process of self-assessment is a learned behavior, and it takes time for students to feel safe about doing this. Initially, students are hesitant to talk about what they did well for fear of "showing off," and they are fearful of pointing out their weaker pieces, in case it lowers the summative value of their portfolios. In responding to what students do well, and by acknowledging the weaknesses in a supportive and nonjudgmental way, I have been able to create an environment where students focus on their growth, rather than on their failures. As one student put it, "The thing I like most about this class is the interactions."

The letters allow students to write about their work and to articulate both their pride and their confusion. This gives me the opportunity to see what I need to remediate in terms of clarifying or reteaching, or even gently scolding. Students, once they feel safe, can be remarkably honest. John, for example, states:

"Students, once they feel safe, can be remarkably honest."

> "Something that I know I have to work on is staying on task with my work. This past quarter wasn't my best and I know I can do better. I also need to write more in my journals. I try to write as much as I can but I write kind of slow and I spend half of the time trying to think of things to write about."

Once I read this letter, I changed my journal procedure to allow more time for the students who needed to think about the topic. Additionally, I moved John to a group that was very self-disciplined and kept an eye on him during individual work time to make sure he stayed on task. John's honest self-assessment about his study habits made it possible for me to shape a better classroom environment for him.

The letter exchange allows students to express concerns about their learning and identify their need areas; this empowers students to focus on their own learning and control their own growth. That students respond to the personalization of instruction is clear from this letter excerpt:

> "I'm glad you told me how to improve my slide analysis because I was starting to think that all my papers were exactly the same and that I didn't change anything, but after I read your letter I tried to change my writing the next time we did a slide analysis. I think I deserve an A for the semester or quarter because I

tried hard this quarter to change and improve. My best writing sample that exemplifies why I should get an A is the Parmigianino: Madonna with the Long Neck. That paper came after I read the letter telling me how to improve myself. I tried my best on that art work, and really put a lot of thought into everything I was explaining."

Empowering students to self-assess their learning creates self-motivated and reflective learners. Instead of trying to meet laundry lists of prescriptive criteria and teacher-directed topics, a supportive environment for students allows for risk taking, self-assessment, and personal growth. Empowered students are concerned with doing their best work and not with the fear of "getting things right." For example, I gave my students a long list of suggested writing responses to the story "Picasso Summer" by Ray Bradbury. Mary did none of the suggested assignments. Instead, she created an alternative ending to the story and then submitted that piece as her suggested best work for summative assessment. She wrote in her letter to me:

"I also wanted to tell you that my "Picasso Summer" essay I chose to do my own thing and so I did an alternative ending but I don't think I cleared with you. I think it looked better than any other thing I tried."

"A supportive environment for students allows for risk taking, self-assessment, and personal growth."

The letter gave Mary the opportunity to contextualize her work and explain the risk she took in changing the parameters of the original assignment. She might not have been so willing to take this risk if she didn't feel intellectually safe in an environment focusing on learning rather than on evaluation.

Letters Take Time, but the Investment Pays Off

Engaging students in a year-long correspondence is time consuming and challenging. However, for me, the outcome is worth the investment. In a world where time is a precious commodity, I give my students the gift of my time and my genuine interest in them as individuals. I respond to, and teach them, as individuals. I carve the necessary hours to do this out of my brutal schedule, even though every year, when I'm halfway through the first gigantic mound of portfolios and pounding out letters at top speed, I start mumbling about how maybe traditional grading is a better idea. However, when the second set of letters comes in, they are filled with personal anecdotes, connections between the curriculum and students' families and histories, insights into the teaching and learning process, self-selected excellent writing, and honest appraisals about work habits, skills deficits, and strengths. Reading those letters, I always celebrate my students' growth and honesty and value their developing ability to discuss their work, while making connections between the curriculum and the real world. I enjoy the friendships that these letters forge, and as a teacher, I am thrilled to see students engaged in their own learning and assessment.

I suppose one of the more important aspects of letter writing for me is that I begin to see my students as people beyond the boundaries of my classroom. From a three-page single-spaced expansive letter by a student exploring her personal history and ideas, with detailed explanations for every assignment, to a minimalist response of one paragraph identifying that "I don't really have any problems with this class," my students expose themselves to me in their letters and remind me that learning is a dynamic and organic activity.

"…and remind me that learning is a dynamic and organic activity."

As a teacher, I always have a plan in mind when I deliver a lesson, but by giving my students a chance to talk to me about those lessons and about their learning, I also open myself up to learning. Learning from my students is what makes the letter writing such a joy. When my students write to me about what they struggled with or what they enjoyed, I always take another look at what I tried to accomplish with a lesson, and just by taking a second or third or fourth look, I am working as a self-reflective practitioner and learner. The letters my students write about their successes and failures in my class serve to amend and drive my approaches to teaching and are instrumental in creating a classroom environment of friendship, collaboration, and trust. Assessment in this paradigm is not just an assigned grade but a force for learning. Most importantly to me as a teacher, the letters I exchange with my students are my window into their world and, for each of them, their window into mine.

References

Atwell, N. (1986). *In the middle: Writing, reading, and learning with adolescents.* Portsmouth, NH: Heinemann.

Inannone, R. V., and Obenauf, P. (1999). Towards spirituality in curriculum and teaching. *Education, 119*(4): 737–751.

Kohn, A. (2000). *The schools our children deserve.* Boston: Houghton Mifflin Company.

Noddings, N. (1999). Caring and competence. In G. Griffin (Ed.), *The education of teachers* (pp. 205–220). Chicago: University of Chicago Press.

Rathyen, C. (2006). *Teacher, teacher, show me a picture: Rethinking English, a practitioner study.* Doctoral dissertation, University of Hawaii, Honolulu. Dissertation Abstracts International PN3216082 (pp. 1675–1924)

Section Three
Preparing to Evaluate and Report

Section Three:
Preparing to Evaluate and Report

Effective classroom assessment supports learning and leads to standards-based reporting that respects the structure of each unique subject area or discipline, supports student learning and achievement, communicates effectively with a range of audiences, *and* fulfills our required legal and regulatory responsibilities. As the following chapters demonstrate, there is not one single right answer, but many right answers that reflect the discipline being taught and the ways of learning and knowing that students need to demonstrate. In this section, these teachers describe how they have effectively worked through complexity to something much, much better—a simple, powerful practice and informed standards-based grading and reporting process. Do not be deceived by the simplicity of these ideas; appreciate the power of them. They are the simplicity found on the far side of complexity.

In summary, after the learning and as teachers move to evaluating and reporting, there are four tasks:

1. Finalize the collection of evidence of learning (including determining the role of formative and summative assessment evidence).
2. Make an informed professional judgment about the quality of the evidence and about where on the continuum of progress toward the standard(s) that work falls.
3. Report using required format (percentages, letter grades, number grades, symbols, comments, or narratives).
4. Involve students in communicating with parents about their learning, and invite parents to request any clarification needed.

As you read, notice the variety of ways teachers are engaging in this work, the varied involvement of students, and the ways they prepare themselves and others to communicate learning, achievement, and progress.

11

Melissa Labbe, a mathematics teacher in Maine, reflects on the inability of single summary grades to represent the breadth and depth of student learning and describes how she assesses students' "mathematical" habits of mind. She also examines the impact of averaging scores from different types of work to determine a final grade, and revamps her record-keeping and grading system so it reflects principles of quality classroom assessment.

12 **Gerald Fussell**, a humanities teacher from Comox, British Columbia, in a chapter titled "'No-Grades' Assessment" explains why refraining from grading of student work during the learning time makes sense in terms of motivation, intellectual curiosity, and long-term learning success. He challenges the use and meaning of percentage and numeric grading, describing practical strategies and resources to focus students on their learning rather than grades, and how he has revamped his grade book around learning outcomes.

13 **Lynne Sueoka**, who teaches freshmen and sophomores in a media communications and technology learning center in Hawaii, focuses on the impact of using portfolio assessment as a communication tool that expands the circle of learning. She describes how her students are using online digital portfolios to share evidence of their learning with teachers, parents, and others.

14 **David Mindorff**, a university preparatory school teacher in Toronto, Ontario, discusses the value of establishing formative classroom assessment practices in an often high-stakes/high-anxiety environment. With his Theory of Knowledge (philosophy) and biology students, he provides evidence of learning from student online discussions, as well as peer and self-assessment. He describes matching the quality of student evidence to descriptions of quality that define the symbols used in final grades.

15 **Stephanie Doane**, a teacher of humanities in Maine, uses assessment practices to support lifelong learning in her social studies classes. She describes how her students produce proof of learning using progress folios, student-involved conferences, and student-set criteria. She also highlights how she provides descriptive feedback, as well as time for students to be reflective, even in an environment of increased testing and reporting in percentage grades.

Melissa Labbe

Melissa Labbe, M.S.Ed., has been teaching middle and high school math for more than fifteen years. She has also taught in a vocational school in the service industry and cooperative education program. Melissa is a participant in the assessment learning team at Deering High School in Maine and has presented at state assessment conferences.

Reflective Assessment in Mathematics
by Melissa Labbe

I've always dreaded the end of the quarter when I have to enter grades for students and parents to view on report cards. How does that one number reflect what the student has truly learned over the last eight weeks? Does his grade reflect his knowledge? Does the exam she took after being ill the previous day reflect her understanding and accomplishment? There has to be a better way to represent what the students have learned. When I make my quarterly report, I need to have confidence that the message I am sending is accurate, that the number I'm putting down is truly reflective of a student's learning, and that I have tangible evidence to support it.

My school district and many others still rely on a numeric reporting system to determine class standing, scholarship eligibility, and course placement for the next semester. The only consistency in reporting is how the numbers are broken down and assigned a grade letter. There is no common practice around the use of rubrics or percentages assigned to various types of work. My goal was to find a way to report students' strengths and weaknesses more accurately.

My first attempt at reporting grades to reflect student learning entailed a high volume of collecting and correcting. I would assign homework, and collect and correct it the next day while we discussed the material in class and did examples on the board at the students' request. This proved both time consuming for me and boring for those students who didn't need the extra examples. Along with the collection of homework, there were quizzes, tests, and projects, which had been assigned various weights, to comprise the students' grades at the end of the semester. I found that some of the grades didn't seem to fit what the student really knew and was demonstrating, so I began to rethink how I set up my grade book.

As I looked at the current structure, it occurred to me that the discrepancy I was seeing was due to the averaging of the practice assignments that was taking place. If I compared students' homework scores to that of their quizzes and tests, they were losing credit for needing more practice.

What I really wanted to capture were the points in time that reflected the students' best work and acquisition of knowledge. I still felt it was important for students to be held accountable for their homework and daily practice, but not to the extent that I currently reported. Therefore, I revamped my grading system to comprise one homework grade that was assigned a lower percentage and was based on their effort on (not necessarily the correctness of) the assignments. This grade, along with the grades from their quizzes, tests, and projects, were averaged to find the overall grade. However, this method didn't give students enough feedback or incentive to complete the practice work outside of class. It also penalized students who didn't need to do the work to master the skill/concept and students who required more practice over time.

"Some of the grades didn't seem to fit what the student really knew and was demonstrating."

Somehow I needed to find a way to value the practice that came with homework so that students would recognize the impact it had on their overall learning. I wanted to track homework behaviors without penalizing students for the amount of time or volume of work they needed to complete. Since I was using an electronic grade book, I was able to make categories that would appear on a report but have no bearing numerically on the students' grades (Figure 1). This is where I decided to put homework.

As students completed homework assignments, I would periodically collect them and give written feedback to the students. If more than half of the problems were attempted or completed, the student received credit for the assignment in my grade book. This allowed me to track which students were doing their assignments and to what extent homework was being completed. As students took quizzes and tests, I could look back at their homework habits and point out to the students how their behavior was impacting their grade. When progress reports were sent out, I was able to attach notes to individual assignments to inform students and parents whether an assignment was late, not done, or missing due to the student's absence. It provided a clear picture of the student's homework history. Having removed numeric grades from the homework category in the program, I was left with averaging the quizzes, tests, and projects the student had completed. Again, this grade reflected more than the

Figure 1 ▼

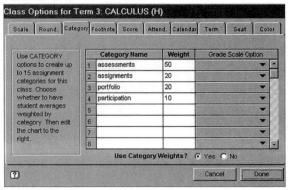

Figure 2 ▼

content knowledge the student had gained. The grades that were entered reflected late penalties for projects not completed by the deadline and potentially lower grades, dragged down by quizzes that were taken before the student fully internalized the concept or skill (Figure 2).

ID	Mis..	Overall	15 of 15 Assignments	Student Questionnaire (participation 2/1/2006)	MI Survey (participation 2/1/2006)	Chapter 1 Exam (assessments 2.1-2.2)	Assessments 2.1-2.2 (assessments 3/7/2006)	5 Additional Limit Prob. (assessments 3/7/2006)	Limits Quiz (assessments 3/10/2006)	Chapter 2 Exam (assessments 3/22/2006)	Spaceship Assessment (assessments 3/27/2006)	Chain Rule Assessment (assessments 3/31/2006)	Chapter 3 exam (assessments 4/7/2006)	Portfolio (portfolio 4/11/2006)
		Overall		100	100	100	44	25	35	66	28	27	79	16
1		89.2 B		cr	cr	92	43	20	35	56	22	24	83	14
2		95.4 A		cr	cr	96	29	23	30	63	24	27	91	16

Again I questioned how I could put down one number that truly represents how close a student is to knowing what is expected at this point in time. In reality, I don't believe that a single number *can* accurately represent a student's acquisition of knowledge, but it is the system under which I work. I decided to adopt Paul Foerster's phrase, "YOU worry about the math, I'LL worry about your grade," to help students keep their focus on the content.

Figure 3 ▼

Students were still responsible for assignments, which were collected randomly. From the start, I told them it was their responsibility to figure out how much practice they needed in order to "get" a concept. I periodically collected their work and made written comments as to what they were doing correctly and what they needed to watch for (such as always dropping a negative sign) (Figure 3).

Now I maintain a homework category in my grade book that is assigned 0% as its weight in the final grade. I track students' quizzes and tests in chronological order by date, categorized by concept. This lets both the students and me see the progress that is made over time. As a student's grade in the quiz/test category improves, it becomes his or her new grade. This allows

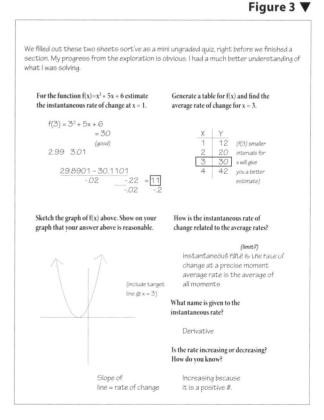

We filled out these two sheets sort've as a mini ungraded quiz, right before we finished a section. My progress from the exploration is obvious. I had a much better understanding of what I was solving.

For the function $f(x)=x^2+5x+6$ estimate the instantaneous rate of change at $x = 1$.

$$f(3) = 3^2 + 5x + 6$$
$$= 30$$
(good)

2.99   3.01

29.8901 – 30.1101
-.02   -.22   = 11
           -.02   -.2

Generate a table for $f(x)$ and find the average rate of change for $x = 3$.

X	Y
1	12
2	20
3	30
4	42

(f(3) smaller intervals for x will give you a better estimate)

Sketch the graph of $f(x)$ above. Show on your graph that your answer above is reasonable.

(include target line @ x = 3)

Slope of line = rate of change

How is the instantaneous rate of change related to the average rates?

(limit?)
instantaneous rate is the rate of change at a precise moment average rate is the average of all moments

What name is given to the instantaneous rate?

Derivative

Is the rate increasing or decreasing? How do you know?

Increasing because it is a positive #.

Figure 4 ▼

Mathematics—Habits of Mind

Criteria	Meets the Standard
Persistence	Student takes time to review work. Student makes several attempts at difficult problems. Student follows through with long-term projects.
Questioning	Student responds thoroughly to questions. Student knows how to ask relevant questions that prompt critical thinking.
Drawing on Past Knowledge and Experience	Student draws insight from what they already know. Student is able to identify what they know, what they need to know, and a process for solutions.
Precision of Language and Thought	Student avoids vague descriptions when specifics are required. Student avoids generalizations that indicate the unknown.

a student who needs more time to master a skill or concept to do so without penalty. In classes that are diverse (typically Algebra I and below), differentiation becomes the key. When they have mastered a concept, students move on to new ones. Warm-ups are used at the beginning of class to give practice to old concepts so that skills are not lost. My grading still reflects students' efforts by identifying the mathematical "habits of mind" (Costa and Kallick, 2000) that I want them to develop.

I choose four habits of mind as the focus for each class. These four vary, depending on the class. A rubric is used so that the students can self-evaluate periodically (Figure 4).

"They were losing credit for needing more practice."

I evaluate the students using the rubric and discuss with them what they could do to move to the desired outcome. A portfolio can be used by students to choose pieces of work that represent their growth in the four areas.

At this point, all of the above information is needed to determine each student's final grade. The components include the grades that refer to the content standards and the grades that refer to the selected guiding principles (habits of mind), along with the final exam grade.

My standing policy is that if the final exam grade is higher than the average of the other assessments, it becomes the final content grade. The remainder of the grade comes from the portfolio assessment, which is made up of a student assessment and teacher evaluation. This assessment piece makes up 20 percent of the student's grade. Attendance and participation in my class must be valued at 10 percent. Here is the big picture of my grading structure:

Assessments (quizzes/tests)	50%
Assignments (in and out of class)	20%
Portfolio	20%
Attendance/Participation	10%

These are the components of the student's quarterly grade. Two quarter grades are then averaged to find the semester grade. This is the point at which I compare the final exam grade to the semester average. Using the larger of the two, 80 percent of that score plus 20 percent of the final portfolio evaluation, makes up the student's final grade.

Although using a single grade to represent a student's acquisition of knowledge and progress still remains an inadequate way to report, I am more satisfied with the assessment process, and the students seem to be more focused on their learning and growth over the course of the semester.

Have all the students enjoyed this process? No. Has it been an easy road? No. In the beginning, colleagues and parents were dubious, but they and the students came to see that I was truly looking for a better way to represent student achievement. As colleagues received my former students, they were able to rely on the marks earned as representative of the student's learning as a whole. Parents had a better understanding of their students' strengths and weaknesses, as did the students themselves. As students became able to articulate and discuss their learning, their focus began to shift. Their grades no longer reflected only whether a course had been completed, but truly represented what had been learned and accomplished.

"Their grades no longer reflected only whether a course had been completed, but truly represented what had been learned and accomplished."

References

Costa, A., and Kallick, B. (2000). *Assessing and reporting on habits of mind.* Alexandria, VA: Association for Supervision and Curriculum and Development.

Foerster, P. (2005). *Calculus: Concepts and applications.* Emeryville, CA: Key Curriculum Press.

Gerald Fussell

Gerald W. Fussell, B.A., B.Ed., M.Ed., has a master's degree in curriculum leadership from the University of Victoria, Canada, and, as a school administrator, he has played a pivotal role in improving schoolwide literacy. His students have profitably published four books, three on British Columbia history, including the award-winning *Blazing Paddles: Historical Fiction of British Columbia.* Gerald has worked with teams of professionals creating curriculum projects and professional development opportunities. In addition to his classroom and school work, he has given presentations at the provincial and national level, and has had numerous essays published in professional journals and public media.

"No-Grades" Assessment
by Gerald Fussell

"Is this for grades?"

With this question, another product of our system demonstrates our failure to teach lifelong learning. We effectively train students to respond to external motivators by creating artificial remuneration—and it *is* artificial. This dependency undermines the joy and passion of learning. When children enter school, they do things out of intellectual curiosity; however, they soon learn to do things only when rewards or punishments are attached. Grades are the product and the genus of this dependency. By shifting to a system that does not use grades, student success is increased because students are connecting the work they are doing to their learning and the learning is being connected to their needs. They have ownership.

> When there were grades, I focused more on my overall grade; I ignored what I needed to work on, and I would just get angry over the fact my grade was low. With the no-grades, I found myself looking for what I needed to work on, and I actually found ways to improve my skills for me. I know what I do well, what I need to work on, and how to get support for my learning. (JL)

My journey to not using grades was precipitated by my desire to extend the effectiveness of my teaching. I began exploring various options when I was teaching English 12. I became increasingly frustrated by the number of repeated writing errors. I was spending considerable time on each paper making many constructive comments, but these comments went largely unheeded. I adopted a policy in my courses that I would write many comments for the first month and then put none on for the remainder of the course. I was nervous the first couple of times I did it, and then I became angry. The students didn't seem to notice that I was not putting comments on their work—or at least they didn't say anything about it. After that, I began to watch what my students did: they got their papers, they looked at their grades, they reacted to their grades, and then they filed their papers in the appropriate receptacle. It seemed that my time spent creating constructive comments had been wasted.

Adding fuel to my antipathy toward grades was my evolving sense that they meant nothing. Notwithstanding the whole discussion about the difference between percentage points—what's the difference between 65 percent and 60 percent other than 5 percentage points?—I began to question the validity in most numeric grading. To my eye, numeric grading, especially in the humanities, was essentially a ranking system akin to the bell curve. What is the difference between the work getting a 7/10 and the work getting an 8/10? Purists will argue that it's the number of errors, or the like; however, I began to question the clarity of my vision. Was I clear about what I was assessing? Was I assessing the number of spelling errors made? Was I tallying the number of fragments? What educational value did my grading have? If I wasn't clear, how could my students understand or value what I was putting on their page? And then, that brought me to letter grades.

"What does the letter grade really mean? Does it mean the same thing to the teacher as it does to the student? Does it mean the same to parents?"

What does the letter grade on a report card mean? Think about that for a minute. What does the letter grade really mean? Does it mean the same thing to the teacher as it does to the student? Does it mean the same to parents? Let's examine how these letter grades are created. Grades are collected—Are grades taken off for late work? How does that accurately reflect understanding? What grade does missing work receive? What's been evaluated? Work habits?—then these same grades are added together, divided by total number available to arrive at a percentage. That percentage fits into a range corresponding to a letter grade that gets placed on a report card. So what does that letter grade tell the parent? Does the student understand the concepts? Which ones? At best, this system ranks the students, as opposed to indicating their potential or ability; it uses competition rather than the establishment of empirical criteria that are understood and explainable. The more I looked at reporting, the more I realized that it meant different things for our different constituents. Thus, I began to question its validity.

Additionally, this system creates and reinforces "pleasers" as opposed to thinkers. Students quickly become focused on their grades, rather than on the learning. They are rewarded for neat coloring and title pages. I found that students would rather write a dry, structurally basic essay than try rhetorical style or narrative essays. When

I asked them why, my top students told me clearly that they knew how to do the basic essay and did not want to lose grades by doing the assignment "wrong."

I was faced with a dilemma: I was not satisfied with the status quo of itemized assessment nor with the status quo of reporting systems, but I was working within a culture that perpetuated itself. Time constraints, accountability pressures, indoctrinated constituents (parents, students, and colleagues), and infrastructure came into conflict with my growing recognition that what I was doing was not nearly as effective as it could, or should, be. My students were not receiving the full value of what I could offer. Something had to give.

I started to look at literature on assessment. It did not take me long to find Grant Wiggins and Jay McTighe (1998). Their book *Understanding by Design* asked and addressed some fundamental questions for me. In essence, it directed me to start with the end in mind and to then work backward. What do we want students to understand and to be able to do? How will we know that they do understand and do have the skills? The point they emphasized that resonated with me was that assessment needed to accurately and clearly inform the student. Jan and Stephen Chappuis (2002) further illuminated the situation for me by writing about the need for assessment to be cognizant of and appropriate for its users. What is needed by whom, and what decisions are going to be made with this information? Marzano's work (2003) demonstrated unequivocally the primary value of immediate feedback: no grades are involved in this. In *Strategies That Work,* Harvey and Goudvis (2000) explained effective strategy after effective strategy, and surprisingly, none of them called for making things worth grades. Nor are grades mentioned as effective by Tovani (2004) or Brownlie et al. (2006). North West Regional Educational Laboratory (NWREL) and North Central Regional Educational Laboratory (NCREL) have done some work examining the adverse effects grades have on learning, but at this point, tangible application in response to the research is minimal. Despite very powerful research showing the importance of assessment *for* learning—as opposed to evaluation *of* learning—done by Fuchs and Fuchs in 1986 as well as Kohn (1993, 2000), Deci, Koestner, and Ryan (1999), and Harlen and ALRSG (2001), little has changed in classroom practice. In 1998, Black and Wiliam reported unequivocally on the importance of formative assessment; however, policy makers continue to invest in evaluation of learning.

> The main plank of our argument is that standards can be raised only by changes that are put into direct effect by teachers and pupils in classrooms. There is a body of firm evidence that formative assessment is an essential component of classroom work and that its development can raise standards

of achievement. We know of no other way of raising standards for which such a strong prima facie case can be made. Our plea is that national and state policy makers will grasp this opportunity and take the lead in this direction. (Black and Wiliam, 1998)

In addition to these works, I have read a number of articles that decried the value of grades. The fire was beginning to smolder.

When grading BC English 12 government final exams, I was first introduced to the concept of coding. We were not putting grades on papers; rather, we were assigning a numeric code to the paper. These codes, one through six, corresponded to descriptors, such as: for poetry, a "five response is proficient and reflects a strong grasp of the topic and the [poem]. The references to the [poem] may be explicit or implicit and convincingly support [the discussion]. The writing is well organized and reflects a strong command of the conventions of language. Errors may be present, but are not distracting" (English, n.d.). From these descriptors and the process flowed many discussions concerning assessment. These were high-stakes decisions that were being made by very conscientious and caring professionals, and accuracy was crucial. Less significant, but philosophically aligned, was the coding being done on the Foundation Skills Assessment. What became clear from these experiences was that the minutia of the numeric grading I was doing in the classroom was not accurate or informative. The smoldering intensified.

"The conversation changed from 'What grade did you give me?' to 'I know I'm fully meeting expectations because …'"

I began dallying with performance standards (http://www.bced.gov.bc.ca/perf _stands/). The descriptors that were used made sense to me, and to my students. Not only did they understand the point-form descriptors, but they understood the four categories: not yet within grade-level expectations, minimally meeting expectations, fully meeting expectations, and exceeding expectations. For each level, the rating scales in writing, for example, give a snapshot description and then more detailed descriptors for meaning, style, form, and conventions. My students were able to describe what work fitting each descriptor looked like. The conversation changed from, "What grade did you give me?" to "I know I'm fully meeting expectations because I can make and support logical interpretations of themes," and "Mr. Fussell, how can I introduce indirect quotes to help my writing become more effective?"

Another benefit of using the performance standards was the ability to monitor, track, and demonstrate growth. The Quick Scales became a very powerful tool that allowed me to get a snapshot of where the students were individually. They show a progression with each level having twelve to fifteen point-form descriptors. For example, at the grade 9 level writing to communicate ideas and information, the descriptors for conveying meaning are shown in Figure 1.

Granted, a glance in my grading records would have told me part of that story; however, the Quick Scales gave me details and clarity that my grading records did not. They did the same for my students. Also, by using different colored highlighters, we were able to see progress made at various checkpoints in the year.

Figure 1 ▼

At first the Quick scales [sic] were hard, but the more we did them, the easier they became. It was cool to see the different colors on the page and to see the way my reading had improved. My sheet became really tattered by the end of the term, but I still have it and look at it every now and then. I wish we were still using them, they really helped. (CB, 2 years later)

This was far more powerful than the standard unit tests, quizzes, and homework checks I used to use because it was consistent, transparent, and made sense to the students. They understood where they were and knew what we were working toward and what

	Not yet within grade level expectations	Minimally meeting grade level expectations	Fully meeting grade level expectations	Exceeding grade level expectations
MEANING • ideas and information • use of detail • use of sources transitions	• purpose may be unclear; focus is not sustained; often very brief	• purpose is clear; focus may lapse in places, often due to ineffective ideas made explicit	• purpose is clear; focus is maintained throughout, with relationships among purpose	• tightly focused, will all material contributing to a well-defined
	• supporting examples and details are often irrelevant, general, or simplistic; it is difficult to follow the writer's reasoning	• some development through relevant examples or details; some unsupported generalizations or illogical reasoning	• carefully and logically developed with relevant examples and details originality	• logically developed with relevant, vivid examples and details; may show
	• information is often incomplete and may be inaccurate; tends to rely on limited sources and not be restated in writer's own words	• information is accurate, but may be incomplete or poorly integrated; draws on appropriate sources	• information is accurate and complete; may integrate information from several appropriate sources	• information is accurate and complete, often skillfully integrated from a variety of appropriate sources
	• little sense of audience; tone may be inappropriate	• some sense of audience; tries to use an appropriate tone	• clear sense of audience; appropriate tone; shows some consideration for the reader	• clear sense of audience; appropriate tone; shows consideration for reader and tries to create an impact (where appropriate)

Figure 1: Rating Scale: Grade 9 Writing to Communicate Ideas and Information

achievement would look like. This assessment focused on assessment *for* learning. Students learned to assess and evaluate their own work with clarity and precision. This, far more than any of my former practices, led to meaningful learning that was owned by the students. The fire was being fanned at this point. Supporting the pedagogy of the performance standards, the three-part series by Gregory, Cameron, and Davies (2011a; 2011b; 2011c) presented methodology for and affirmation of my desire to go gradeless.

From this, the system evolved. The language we (my students, their parents, other teachers of the same students, and I) use revolves around meeting the grade-level expectations (established through published performance indicators, Quick Scales, and experience) with respect to the learning outcomes for each course. This has posed problems and some discomfort for subsequent teachers. Assignments do not receive grades; they receive comments, suggestions, and modifications. The students read these; the students understand these; the students learn from these. The feedback is very much focused on assessment *for* learning. My comments focus on ways the students can improve technically, stylistically, and/or intellectually as opposed to being judgmental or evaluative. Also, by removing the stigma of grades, students were encouraged to take risks and responsibility for their own learning. "Why work on your slap-shot at practice when your wrist-shot is much weaker?" became their unofficial mantra. By demystifying the process, I have also been able to get the students to use assessment *for* learning. They can effectively establish their own criteria and clearly assess their own work. While I still serve as the fountain of knowledge, the role has shifted from punitive to supportive; from the distributor of grades to the distributor of knowledge and skills. I like the new job description; it fits more accurately the ideals with which I entered this profession.

Figure 2 ▼

Assignment 1	Assignment 2	Assignment 3	Assignment 4	Assignment 5	Assignment 6	
√	√√	√√	√	√	√√	A
√√	√	√	√√	√√	~	B
~	√	√	√	~	√	B
X	√		~	~	~	C
√√	~	X	~	~		C-
	X		X	~		F

√√ = Exceeds expectations   ~= Minimally meets expectations
√ = Fully meets expectations   X= Not within grade level expectations

Assignments:
1 = Initial writing assessment   2 = Explanation of concept "revolution"
3 = Research paper on Industrial Revolution   4 = Web-quest on Industrial Revolution
5 = Section questions from textbook   6 = Comparison of primary and secondary documents

Social Studies 9—Intended Learning Outcomes—Samples
It is expected that students will:
- Analyze the factors that contribute to revolution and conflict
- Analyze the contributions of the English, French, and American revolutions in the development of democratic concepts
- Identify and clarify a problem, an issue, or an inquiry
- Select and summarize information from primary and secondary print and nonprint sources, including electronic sources
- Assess the reliability, currency, and objectivity of different interpretations of primary and secondary sources
- Plan, revise, and deliver formal oral and written presentations
- Identify factors that influenced growth and development of industry
- Evaluate the effects of the Industrial Revolution on society and the changing nature of work

My "grading records" contain symbols—blank for not handed in, *X* for not within grade-level expectations, squiggly line for minimally meeting expectations, a √ for fully meeting expectations, and √√ for exceeding expectations.

Figure 2 shows an example of my grades from term 1 in Social Studies 9.

There are some assignments (2, 3, 6) that I design specifically to demonstrate achievement of learning outcomes; there are some assignments (1, 4, 5) that I have given to provide me information or breathing room, or to reinforce skills knowledge (i.e., chapter questions, worksheets, and so on). The symbols for the former supersede in value the symbols for the latter, and an appropriate letter grade is assigned. Even in this last scenario, the students understand their "grade" and can explain why it is an accurate reflection of their achievement. Students know, with every assignment, how they are doing relative to the grade-level expectation, and our discussions about their work are meaningful and efficient. There are no surprises at the end of a term.

At the end of each term, students write a summary that must include their goals related to the learning outcomes for the course, how they achieved their goals, and what they plan to work on next term. These summaries are attached to the appropriate report cards. By doing this, the focus is on the learning outcomes.

> *This term we explored population trends, the British Revolution, and the Industrial revolution (sic) to work on numerous learning outcomes for Social Studies 9. . . . By working on the term papers on the Industrial Revolution, I used primary and secondary documents, assessed their relative values, and selected what information to include and what information was not necessary to my plan. The term paper also allowed me to work on the learning outcomes for preparing and presenting information to support a point or issue. . . . I still need to work on understanding the impact of these European events on North America, but Mr. Fussell has assured me that we will be doing that next term.* (TR)

"What about those students who, on hearing there are no grades, won't do any work?"

The grade that appears on the report card reflects the symbols in my grading records, their summary, and our understanding. When I glance across a line and see a series of double checks, I know that person is exceeding grade-level expectations, thus an *A* appears on her report card. When I see a series of X's, I know that she is not meeting grade-level expectations and an *I* appears on her report card with an alternate plan to have her demonstrate her proficiency. In reality, on the last example, I've been in contact with home on numerous occasions, and supports are in place; however, all parties involved understand that the grade represents the student's present demonstration of learning outcomes. Now, where it gets tricky is when there exists a variety of symbols across a given line. In this case, I look at the various symbols for various assignments, cognizant of the relative importance of each to the learning outcomes.

So what are the pitfalls? What about those students who, on hearing there are no grades, won't do any work? What about late assignments? What about the numeric-based grades programs? The students who, on hearing there are no grades, decide to do no work are the same ones who regularly don't hand in work even when it is for grades, and are often late with assignments they do hand in. What I have found is that with the shift of focus to their learning and their need to meet the learning outcomes, the onus falls on them, and the number of assignments missing or carelessly done is reduced considerably. With one of my classes, I used grades in the first term and approximately 30 percent of the students received failing grades, due in large part to missing assignments. In the second term, I went to the no-grade system, and all but one demonstrated acceptable proficiency of the learning outcomes. When I asked them why the change occurred, the most common response was that they had not previously connected that the work they were doing was for their learning.

Late assignments will always be a burden to us; however, I have never seen how reducing a grade because an assignment is late is an accurate reflection of the student's ability, proficiency, or knowledge. Also, in tracking my myriad late policies over the years, I found that I was doing more work than my students. With the no-grade system, the focus becomes more on demonstrating learning than it does on deadlines. Granted, I am in contact with parents pretty quickly if a student has a couple of assignments missing; however, I do not feel it is reasonable to expect that all students can complete the same tasks in the same time frame. By not assigning grades, I have been able to get away from the conundrums connected with late assignments.

"With the no-grade system, the focus becomes more on demonstrating learning than it does on deadlines."

I have never been one to accept systemic factors overriding pedagogy. Electronic grades programs are tools to be used and have very valuable and important purposes. However, all grades programs can be manipulated to meet our needs. At first I overrode the program and manually entered the letter grade rather than having the computer do it. With another program, I was not able to do that, so I entered one grade each term; however, the grade carefully reflected the letter grades: exceeding expectations = 90 percent; fully meeting expectations = 80 percent; minimally meeting expectations = 60 percent; not yet meeting expectations = 40 percent. I have to admit, I did use 70 percent and 100 percent on several occasions. I don't know about other jurisdictions, but in mine, percentage grades are only, by law, to be used in grades 10 through 12; grades 4 through 9 are to use letter grades only, and the descriptors align with the language of assessment I use.

When I have worked with grades 10 through 12, and have had to report percentages, I have changed my system only slightly. Instead of using the visual codes, I use numeric equivalents: 1 = not yet within grade-level expectations; 2 = minimally meeting grade-level expectations; 3 = fully meeting grade-level expectations; and 4 = exceeding grade-level expectations. These numeric symbols are applied to each of the learning outcomes for the course. These descriptors line up with the descriptors for letter grades.

A The student demonstrates excellent or outstanding performance in relation to the learning outcomes for the course or subject and grade.

B The student demonstrates very good performance in relation to the learning outcomes for the course or subject and grade.

C+ The student demonstrates good performance in relation to the learning outcomes for the course or subject and grade.

C The student demonstrates satisfactory performance in relation to the expected learning outcomes for the course or subject and grade.

C- The student demonstrates minimally acceptable performance in relation to the learning outcomes for the course or subject and grade.

F Failed or failing. The student has not demonstrated, or is not demonstrating, minimally acceptable performance in relation to the learning outcomes for the course or subject and grade. The letter grade *F* may only be assigned if an *I* (In Progress) letter grade has been previously assigned for that course or subject and grade or if the *F* is assigned as a result of failing a provincially examinable course.

These descriptors are aligned to the following numeric equivalents set by the province (http://www.bced.gov.bc.ca/reportcards/reporting_student_progress.pdf): 86–100 (*A*); 73–85 (*B*); 67–72 (*C+*); 60–66 (*C*); 50–59 (*C-*); 0–49 (*F*). Consequently, if a student has consistently (i.e., three-fourths of the time) exceeded grade-level expectations, they will get a "high *A*" (94 percent). If they have an equal combination of learning outcomes they've partially met and fully met, they will end up with 68 percent or a *C+* meaning "[T]he student demonstrates good performance in relation to [the] . . . learning outcomes for the course or subject and grade" (B.C. Ministry of Education, 2012). If the student were to fully meet all learning outcomes for a course, they would receive 80 percent or a *B* meaning "[T]he student demonstrates very good performance in relation to [the] . . . learning outcomes for the course or subject and grade" (B.C. Ministry of Education, 2012).

Part of the beauty of this system is that the expectations are transparent and the evaluation genuinely shared, putting the responsibility on the students, especially at the upper grade levels, to demonstrate their proficiency.

One of the significant drawbacks that I have not yet successfully navigated is the intermediate reporting. While this system works very well for final reports, what about the reports for terms 1 and 2 if on a linear system? It does not seem right to me to be expecting mastery of many learning outcomes, especially skills-based learning, prior to a final report. What would an *A* mean if given at the end of term 1—in relation to learning outcomes that build throughout the year? What would falling grades indicate? Does one necessarily begin with grades representing partial or minimal grade-level achievement (i.e., *C* and *C-*)? Do we evaluate based on grade-level expectations relative to where the class is in the course, such as, "for one-third of the way through English 11 you should be able to . . ."?

I believe this system to be less of a problem in building-block courses such as math, science, and possibly social studies; however, it is particularly problematic in English language arts, languages, and physical education (though with the move to more constructivist pedagogy and cyclical approaches to math, it quickly falls into the second category). In these cases, I have assigned grades based on my expectations for where students should be at a specific point in the course. Obviously, learning outcomes that will not be revisited later carry a lot of weight; however, as a teacher, I feel that my expectations of appropriate progress are valid and I feel confident to report on achievement relative to where we are in the course.

"Like any change, it was not smooth and easy. However, the results, even in that first class, validated the shift."

To take the plunge did not take courage; it took conviction. And like any change, it was not smooth and easy. However, the results, even in that first class, validated the shift. The following comments are by grade 9 students, written on their year-end evaluations. At the end of each term, the students were asked to write a one-page summary of the term—what they'd improved upon; how and what they still needed to work on—and these were attached to their report cards. On this last evaluation, I'd asked for a summative paragraph about the course and the impact of not using grades. In some cases I have summarized, in their words, parts of other written and oral evaluations they have done.

> *Not knowing our grades all of the time made the pressure less intense. I was able to take risks without worrying about how it would affect my grade: I was able to try things to improve my skills.* (CD)

> *The "No-Grades" system inspired students to do their best, even though there were no traditional rewards: we were rewarded solely by our own learning. Once I got past the procrastination piece and realized I needed to demonstrate my achievement of the ILOs, I learned more than I ever have in a class.* (ZM)

I participated more, much more. (RH)

I was challenged in ways no class has challenged me before. I have grown phenomenally over the last year in many aspects, and am much more proud of my grades. . . . One of the unique aspects of this course was the fact there were no formal grades written on assignments. This allowed me to open up, and say what I really thought and pour my soul into what I did because I didn't have to worry about it being right or wrong. I didn't have to think constantly about whether or not what I was writing would get a check mark; I only had to consider if it was what I really thought and if what I was writing was improving my communication skills. I think it took so much pressure off the entire class, when we weren't constantly worrying about how our grades would tally up in the end and effect the all important "letter." Without that pressure we could do our best on the projects laid out for us. (RS)

I know what I do well, what I need to work on, and how to get support for my learning. I did not like not having grades at first, because I felt lost at where I was, grade wise. As the year went on, I adjusted and I actually like it now. When there were grades, I focused more on my overall grade; I ignored what I needed to work on, and I would just get angry over the fact my grade was low. With the no-grades, I found myself looking for what I needed to work on, and I actually found ways to improve my skills for me. I also learned to let others in my class edit my work with me. (JL)

It gets rid of the gloating that so often occurs amongst classmates, especially by the "pleasers." . . . Since I came into this class, I have regained my interest in school. . . . I have gained writing skills, planning skills, research skills, critical thinking skills, and an incredible amount of general knowledge. . . . We were acknowledged for our thoughts and our growth as opposed to how neatly we colored the proverbial map. . . . Even peer editing worked well, we were open to support as opposed to defensive and the editors actually gave honest feedback as opposed to ego stroking. (RC)

I read the comments for the first time in my school life and learned from them. (JC)

I have also received many comments from other teachers and former students that confirm the value of "no-grades" based on the subsequent performance of my students.

Not without its difficulties, the system that I employ addresses many of the concerns I had with evaluation. The students are responsible for their learning; I am not the sole purveyor of mystical judgment and validation. The evaluation reflects the prescribed learning outcomes and is understood by all user groups. The efforts I expend on my evaluation translate directly and effectively into learning for my students. The time I spend on grading and reporting has been reduced, while exponentially increasing in power. My students take risks, push themselves, hold me accountable through their questions and our discussions, and understand what they are doing and why. But, above all else, the reason I am a proponent of this system is that my students excel by all measures in their subsequent, related pursuits. The growth they show while with me is continued after they leave my classroom. Most importantly, to my eye, their attitudes toward the learning have changed; they are responsible for their own learning and they know it. Now I'm truly working to develop lifelong learners.

References

B. C. Ministry of Education. (2012). Provincial letter grades order. http://www.bced.gov.bc.ca/legislation/schoollaw/e/m192-94.pdf

Black, P., and Wiliam, D. (1998). Inside the black box: Raising standards through classroom assessment. *Assessment in Education, 5*(1), 139–144, 146–148. http://www.pdkintl.org/kappan/kbla9810.htm

Brownlie, F., Feniak, C., and Schnellert, L. (2006). *Student diversity: Classroom strategies to meet the learning needs of all students.* Markham, ON: Pembroke Publishers Ltd.

Chappuis, J., and Chappuis, S. (2002). *Understanding school assessment.* Portland, OR: Assessment Training Institute, Inc.

Deci, E. L., Koestner, R., and Ryan, R. M. (1999). A meta-analysis review of experiments examining the effects of extrinsic rewards on intrinsic motivation. *Psychological Bulletin, 125,* 627–668.

English 12—1208 Form A Scoring Guide. (n.d.). http://www.bced.gov.bc.ca/exams /search/grade12/english/release/key/1112en_pk.pdf

Fuchs, L. S., and Fuchs, D. (1986). Effects of systematic formative evaluation: A meta-analysis. *Exceptional Children, 53*(3), 199–208.

Gregory, K., Cameron, C., and Davies, A. (2011a). *Conferencing and reporting* (2nd ed.). Bloomington, IN: Solution Tree Press.

Gregory, K., Cameron, C., and Davies, A. (2011b). *Self-assessment and goal setting* (2nd ed.). Bloomington, IN: Solution Tree Press.

Gregory, K., Cameron, C., and Davies, A. (2011c). *Setting and using criteria* (2nd ed.). Bloomington, IN: Solution Tree Press.

Harlen, W., and the Assessment and Learning Research Synthesis Group (ALRSG). (2001). *The impact of summative assessment and tests on pupils' motivation for learning* (review). http://eppi.ioe.ac.uk/EPPIWebContent/reel/review_groups/assessment /assessment_protocol1.pdf

Harvey, S., and Goudvis, A. (2000). *Strategies that work*. Markham, ON: Pembroke Publishers Ltd.

Kohn, A. (1993). *Punished by rewards*. Boston: Houghton Mifflin.

Kohn, A. (2000). *The case against standardized testing*. Portsmouth, NH: Heinemann.

Marzano, R. J. (2003). *What works in schools: Translating research into action*. Alexandria, VA: Association for Supervision and Curriculum Development.

North Central Regional Educational Laboratory (NCREL). http://www.ncrel.org/

North West Regional Educational Laboratory (NWREL). http://www.nwrel.org/

Tovani, C. (2000). *I read it, but I don't get it: Comprehension strategies for adolescent readers*. Portland, ME: Stenhouse Publishers.

Tovani, C. (2004). *Do I really have to teach reading: Content comprehension grades 6–12*. Portland, ME: Stenhouse Publishers.

Wiggins, G., and McTighe, J. (1998). *Understanding by design*. Alexandria, VA: Association for Supervision and Curriculum Development.

Lynne Sueoka

Lynne Sueoka, B.Ed., M.Ed., is a teacher and staff developer at Moanalua High School in Hawaii. She has attained National Board Certification in the language arts and has been featured in the *Future of Learning* video series I and II, as well as in a video produced by the George Lucas Educational Foundation. Lynne is currently teaching full-time and pursuing doctoral studies in curriculum and instruction.

A Culture of Learning: Building a Community of Shared Learning Through Student Online Portfolios

by Lynne Sueoka

Introduction

My greatest joy in teaching is in planning for new units: figuring out how to approach different concepts, engage the students, and construct practice and project work that would allow for creativity, while providing evidence of learning. However, the grading at the end of the unit has always felt like an exercise in futility: laboring over the comments on each student product, to which few students ever responded. The only thing that counted was the arbitrary numbers, tabulated and averaged over the year into an absurd representation of their learning. Thus, I began my journey toward implementation of portfolio assessment.

It started off as an inquiry into assessment, but in the process, I came to realize that the essence of the portfolio is communication—student to teacher, student and teacher to parents, students and class to the outside world. As the students articulate their learning to these varied audiences and in these varied contexts, they bring meaning and ownership to the process. And through these ever-widening circles of communication, a learning community and a culture of learning are established.

Portfolio Process

For five years now, I have taught freshmen and sophomores in the Media Communications and Technology Learning Center (dubbed MeneMAC after the school's mascot, the Hawaiian menehune). The freshmen enroll in an integrated program of courses, including English, social studies, science, and technology. The sophomores take English, science, and a social studies course with an embedded technology credit. The students are quite media literate and adapt well to the process of documenting their learning electronically.

Figure 1 ▼

Language Arts Grade 9: Spring Semester, 2006—Third Quarter

Standards Addressed	Class Activities	Culminating Assessments
READING STANDARDS	**Writing Focus**	**Journal Assessment #4 (100 points)**
		DUE: Wednesday, March 8, 2006
Vocabulary & Concept Development: Use new grade-appropriate vocabulary, including content area vocabulary, learned through reading and word study	Daily journal exercise	Select two journal entries - one literary and one personal - and develop them into full essays. In
Constructing Meaning: Use annotation methods to identify organizational patterns and to make inferences while reading	Diction and sentence structure	addition, write a final reflection that documents your
Interpretive Stance: Use textual evidence (e.g., knowledge of rhetorical and literary devices)	Critical and interpretive stance responses to class novel and non-fiction texts	process and progress in writing this quarter. This culminating activity will address standards of
to interpret and draw conclusions about literature	Literary Elements	vocabulary, literary elements, range of writing,
Critical Stance: Explain how historical and cultural information enriches the interpretation of a text		sentence structure and grammer, punctuation, capitalization and spelling citing sources, design,
Literary Elements: Analyze the way literary elements and forms are used in prose and poetry	Grammar exercises: online BigDog's Grammar website	and on paperclarity, and voice.
Personal Connection: Explain how literature can deepen and broaden personal experiences and give insight into problems or issues	Grammar Bytes website	**Perspective Poetry (50 points)**
		DUE: Friday, February 24, 2006
WRITING STANDARDS		Write a poem that takes a creative perspective and offers new insight on an issue facing the world
	Writing concepts and exercises: Lively Art of Writing	today. Using Photoshop, create a multi-layered
Range of Writing: Write in a variety of grade-appropriate formats for a variety		graphic that effectively communicates and
of purposes and audiences, such as:	Chapter 5, "First Steps Toward Style"	complements your poem. Write a reflection on your
• Literary, persuasive, and personal essays	Chapter 9, "The Sound of Sentences"	use of poetic techniques and your process of learning about this issue,
• Narratives or scripts with a theme and details that contribute to a mood or tone		composing the poem,
• Poems using a range of poetic techniques and figurative language in a variety of forms	Vocabulary journal *Time* magazine	creating the graphic (minimum 1 page reflection).
• Research papers that state and support a thesis		This culminating activity will address standards of vocabulary,
• Pieces to reflect on learning and to solve problems		interpretive stance, literary elements,
		personal connection, range of writing, meaning,
		design, and clarity
Sentence Structure and Grammar: Form and use the following grammatical constructions correctly when editing writing:	**Literature Focus**	**Scientific Movie Review (100 points)**
		Presentation/ Project DUE: Monday, March 20, 2006
• Parallel structure in various contexts (i.e., items in a series, items juxtaposed for emphasis)	Short story	**(Exam Day)**
	"Dark They Were, and	After watching "The Day After Tomorrow" and
• Subordination and coordination to indicate relationship between ideas	Golden-Eyed" in	reading articles about the science involved in the
• Restrictive clauses with appropriate use of "that"	*A Medicine for Melancholy*	story, select another science fiction film in small
• Abbreviations used in research citation	by Ray Bradbury	groups, vie the film, research the science involved
Punctuation, Capitalization, and Spelling: Edit writing to correct punctuation:	"There Will Come Soft Rains"	and present a scientific panel discussion supporting or refuting
• Ellipsis	By Ray Bradbury in Platinum	the science in the fiction.
• Italics, underlining for foreign words	anthology	This culminating activity will address standards of
Citing Sources: Use a prescribed documentation style to adhere to	"The Pedestrian" by Ray	constructing meaning, interpretive stance, critical citing sources,
fair use and copyright guidelines for citing	Bradbury in *Write On*	discussion and presentation, and media comprehension
grade-appropriate sources in papers, projects, and multimedia presentations		and interpretation.
Citing Sources: Use quotations and citations in writing while	Poetry	
maintaining the flow of ideas	Reading and discussion	**Outside Reading (25 points)**
Meaning: Use accurate and useful research information in writing	(responses also in daily	**DUE: Titles read by February 17 for Scholastic Classrooms**
Design: Use a variety of structural patterns and transitional devices to organize writing	journal exercises)	**Care program; final reflection due on exam day.**
Clarity: Use a variety of sentence structures and grade-appropriate vocabulary to	Literary elements (point of view,	Read and reflect on a science fiction novel.
achieve efficiency, indicate emphasis, clarify meaning	tone, irony, mood, imagery):	This culminating activity will address the standards of critical stance.
Voice: Use a voice and tone appropriate for the topic, purpose, and audience	"Southbound on the Freeway,"	
	"Earth, Earth," "There Will Come	**Standards Portfolio (50 points)**
ORAL COMMUNICATION STANDARDS	Soft Rains," "War"	**CONFERENCE: Thursday, March 16, 2006**
		This is your chance to document how you have met the
Discussion and Presentation: Organize and participate in a small group to	Film	standards for this class. It is an important piece of work as
accomplish a task or explore a topic	*The Day After Tomorrow*	it should augment and add depth to the rest of your
Discussion and Presentation: Give a planned oral presentation highlighting a		"body of work" for this quarter. Pick three of the standards for
main idea(s) with support (e.g., statistics, anecdotes, examples)		which you think you need additional documentation, beyond
Media Comprehension and Interpretation: Describe how images and sound		the culminating activities. Then, provide artifacts and annotation
convey messages in visual media		that show you have genuinely met these standards.

Standards Portfolio

Students are required to compile a digital portfolio for each quarter. The first three portfolios are organized by content areas and their respective standards. At the start of each quarter, the students are given a chart that I have designed following the "backwards mapping" process of McTighe and Wiggins (1998) (Figure 1).

This chart is divided into three columns. The first column lists the standards addressed for the quarter. The second column lists the class assignments and activities that will scaffold the learning. And the final column describes the culminating assessments that will be used for the summative evaluation and grading.

Figure 2 ▼

As they progress through the quarter, the students use a standards worksheet to jot down possible artifacts that they might cite to show attainment of the various standards (Figure 2). In the final weeks of the quarter, they begin their documentation of their learning, coding their text and images in HTML and linking all of the evidence: Word documents, forum posts, images, QuickTime videos, PowerPoints, and others.

mene MAC mohs media communications & technology learning center
www.mohs.k12.hi.us/media-central
Mene MAC Learning Center General Learner Outcomes Worksheet

Name: _____

The Six Hawaii General Learner Outcomes & Your Notes About Them	Possible Artifact/Evidence & Annotation
1. Be responsible for one's own learning	my portfolio because I had to find my own examples to prove my learning and I had to learn the web page coding on my own
2. Understand that it is essential for human beings to work together	sci-fi movie project because we had to do our own research and review and then had to put it all together with the rest
3. Be involved in complex thinking and problem solving	eCybermission would be a good example because we had to follow the scientific method through several steps and check our data and process
4. Recognize and produce quality performance and quality products	the writing self assessments showed this esp the perspectives poem because we looked at examples of poetic techniques and then had to apply them in our own writing

Rather than addressing all the benchmarks for that particular quarter, I guide the students to select the standards that they feel need more supporting evidence than they have been able to provide in the quarterly culminating projects. Thus, Rachael, who had struggled with comprehension and literary analysis all year, elected to provide another essay, analyzing an outside reading novel to demonstrate her attainment of the standard. She reported:

> *The standard that I've tried to reach is INTERPRETIVE STANCE—Use textual evidence (e.g., knowledge of rhetorical and literary devices) [Benchmark:] To interpret and draw conclusions about literature. I*

tried to reach this standard by writing an essay that proves that I understood the book "Shades Children." This book was very interesting to read.

Students upload their completed portfolios to individual online accounts on a Department of Education server and send me their URLs via email so that I may link their portfolios to our learning center site. Then they schedule appointments with parents or guardians, create a portfolio conference agenda, and share their learning. When the parent conference is completed, the students guide their parents or guardians to our learning center forum, where they are asked to share their perceptions of their children's learning.

The following Letter to Parents (see Figure 3) shows the welcome message that appears on the portfolio commentary forum.

Figure 3 ▼

> Dear Parents of the Class of '09,
>
> Thank you for taking the time to share in your children's learning. Please help us to improve that learning experience by posting to this forum.
>
> Our MeneMAC ninth graders will be making an appointment for a sharing session with you and preparing an agenda for that session.
>
> After they share their portfolios with you, they will ask you to share your own reflections about their learning on this forum.
>
> Please note that during this first sharing some of the portfolios may be hard copy and others may be online. We are trying to give our first-time webmasters more time to learn HTML coding and to become comfortable in sharing in the online environment. Second quarter portfolios should all be online.
>
> 1. Please share a little of the discussion that you have had about the learning standards and about how your children have documented them in their portfolios.
>
> 2. Does the portfolio help to give you a better idea of your children's learning? What features of the portfolio have been most helpful and how? In what ways could the portfolio be improved as a tool with which to communicate about your child's learning?
>
> Thank you for supporting your child's learning experience in MeneMAC!!!

> *"It is so different from the point rationing and number crunching of my earlier years in teaching."*

The final step is the conference with me. It is so different from the point rationing and number crunching of my earlier years in teaching. I thoroughly enjoy it and I think my students do, too. They can't stick a crumpled essay under a stack of others and slink out of the room unnoticed. They are literally in the driver's seat, as I have them navigate through the portfolio, while I ask questions to clarify and provide reflection of my own to celebrate their learning. No one asks, "What's my grade?" and I am even able to allow further revision. Because the portfolio is electronic and accessible from home, I can go back and check to see whether a student has put forth that extra effort to improve his or her documentation.

Presentation Portfolio

The final quarter portfolio, the presentation portfolio, requires students to again select and annotate their own artifacts, verifying their attainment of the six general learner outcomes for the state. Unlike the previous portfolios, this one has no subject area designations and students are told to select, from all of their learning experiences, a variety of artifacts that best validates their progress.

The Hawaii State General Learner Outcomes (GLO)

1. Be responsible for one's own learning.
2. Understand that it is essential for human beings to work together.
3. Be involved in complex thinking and problem solving.
4. Recognize and produce quality performance and quality products.
5. Communicate effectively with a variety of audiences for a variety of purposes.
6. Use a variety of technologies effectively and ethically.

   (See References for web address.)

Students follow a similar process, except that this time they have a wider range of activities and artifacts from which to choose. And I urge them to provide multiple artifacts as evidence. Thus, Chanelle highlighted her work in the music program, citing her initiative in working with her clarinet section leader outside of class to validate her attainment of GLO 1, "Be responsible for one's own learning." Several students added their participation in our Learning Center Orientation Night, in which they shared their learning experience with incoming freshmen and their parents, about 60+ students and adults, as evidence that they had attained GLO 5, "Communicate effectively with a variety of audiences for a variety of purposes."

This final portfolio, with its more direct connections to skills and understandings that reach beyond the classroom, becomes a very satisfying end to the year. It doesn't get much better than this post from Laurel:

> *Although I'm not the most comfortable working with Final Cut Pro and other programs, I have accomplished A LOT this past school year. I must say that my skills (or lack of skills) were greatly improved on and many new skills were also acquired. Looking back at all my experiences this past year has made me more eager to continue on in my high school life and my life of gaining neverending knowledge.*

Results: Increased Confidence and Depth of Learning

After using student portfolios for five years, I have found that they result in a greater sense of confidence in the learners, a personal voice that can be heard as students describe their progress though the year, and a sense of a genuine audience to whom they are demonstrating their learning and their pride.

This audience comprises not only the students' parents or guardians, but also includes their peers. In the weeks prior to each portfolio assessment, the classroom hums with students assisting each other in HTML coding, uploading, graphics, and all the other tasks of creating and publishing their online portfolios.

Laurel, a perceptive and articulate ninth grader who succeeded in her academics with ease, was first daunted by her inexperience with web page design and construction. She persevered, determined to master this new skill, and her confidence and success is evident in her fourth quarter presentation portfolio:

"In addition to their emerging sense of self as learners, students show deepened understanding of the concepts covered throughout the year."

> *You know how mother birds push their young birds out of the nests for them to fly? Making a portfolio was the thing that pushed me off the edge to be responsible for my own learning. At first, I fell . . . but I was able to get back up and FLY. . . . I'm really satisfied with my GLO presentation portfolio this quarter because I think it truly expresses how I was before and how I've changed after my freshman year. If you haven't noticed, you can see that my background from the GLO introduction page has gone from a "I DON'T KNOW" mood to a beautiful "I'm confident" mood in my GLO conclusion page (pretty smart huh? Haha.).*

The sophomores added a layer of complexity to their portfolios by creating visual metaphors to communicate their learning. Sharlene used a mirror to convey both her portfolio theme and the overarching theme of the year, identity and one's role in the world.

> *I come in all shapes and sizes. I can be broken very easily and yet I'm as strong as they come. I am a mirror. People see me, but sometimes they don't. They think they see me, but in reality they see what they want to see. They might see themselves, they might see someone else, or they might see something completely off, but what they don't realize is all they're looking at is me.*

Sharlene went on in her portfolio introduction to reflect on the "enduring knowledge" that she had gained from her studies throughout the year. She had become serenely confident of the big picture that goes beyond the "technological and accreditable [sic] portions" of her learning.

> *Even though the technological and accreditable portions of my learning are very important, I feel other things that I have learned that are just as important are the aspects of human nature, mythology and how they relate to us, and other things such as coming of age and the roots of humanity.*

In addition to their emerging sense of self as learners, students show deepened understanding of the concepts covered throughout the year. Part of the portfolio process involves selecting the best artifact for each of the standards or GLOs. Hearing the students explain their selection process helps me to know whether students have understood the skill or concept. As we conference, they sometimes realize that their documentation needs revision, so they agree to put in the added effort, emailing me to check the revision when it is complete.

When we conferenced on GLO 3, "Be involved in complex thinking and problem solving," some students presented math problems as their evidence. Those who could explain that a particular problem or problem series actually involved more than mere computation were accepted. Those for whom "problem solving" meant finding the answers on a worksheet were asked to find better examples of complexity. Most students, however, selected eCybermission, a highly authentic and complex project that required students to solve a real-world problem in their local community, using the scientific method. Joanna used her eCybermission evidence to distinguish between "just solving" and "complex thinking and problem solving." She differentiated complex thinking as a multistep process.

Figure 4 ▼

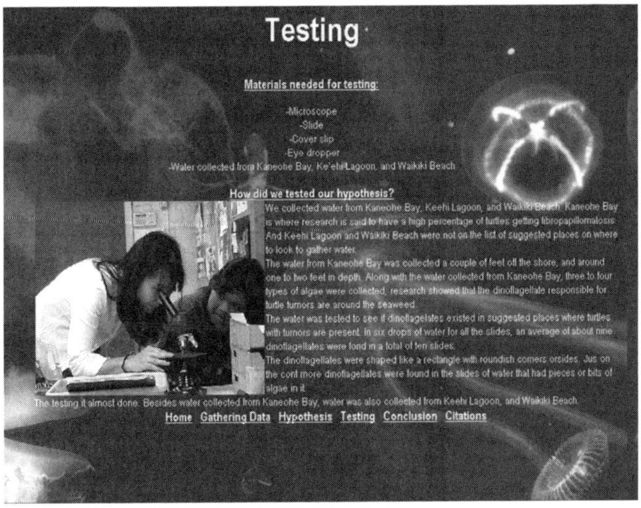

There's a difference between thinking and just solving, to complex thinking and problem solving. The idea of complex thinking isn't a one step process, but involves many steps in order to problem solve (these 2 things go hand in hand). . . . You needed to think of a problem and how you would come about solving it. Now you can't just think of any old problem that you wish, it had to be an actual environmental problem that affected the community.

The next step would be that you had to come up with a reasonable way of solving it, and testing those possible solutions. If that solution didn't work, you have to go back to your collected data to see what went wrong, and then carefully examine it to see how you would test it again, so that it does work.

Laurel demonstrated her understanding that finding the problem, one that was both authentic and solvable, required the greatest thought.

Surprisingly, I think that the most complex thinking done for eCybermission was just thinking of a problem. Surprising huh? There are so many problems in the world and our group couldn't think of one we could use.

She elaborated on her explanation during our portfolio conference, detailing the need for problem validity and the issues of finding the appropriate data-gathering techniques for their hypothesis.

Katreina used a language arts project, Evaluating the Science in Science Fiction, as her example of the complexity of reading and thinking skills necessary to successful completion of the project:

Complex thinking is like extreme thinking, like looking through all points of a subject. This GLO deals with the ability to think at an expanded range and solve problems. . . . For the Scifi movie review project we watched "I, ROBOT" (a science fiction movie). Then we needed to find the scientific theories within the movie and research it to see if it's possible. The research goes under complex thinking. For this project it was essential that you knew what to research and could infer fact from fiction.

Chelsea, a thoughtful and hard-working student, experienced difficulty with her reading and writing skills during our literature-intensive third quarter. She emerged with the hard-won knowledge that sometimes the best knowledge is knowing your own weaknesses, and that learning to learn was the ultimate goal.

> After doing that part of the Journal Assessment, we had to reflect on ourselves as learners and writers. I think that part was important because I had to think about myself and learn my strengths and weaknesses. I met GLO 1 because I had to learn not only about the content, but about myself.

Parent Sharing—The Community Expands

Like our students, our parents are a diverse bunch, unified by their strong desire to support the learning of their children. One example is Melissa's folks, who are graphic designers themselves and whose involvement in her learning Melissa describes in this way:

> For my parent or parents at home presentation, I really didn't need to schedule a specific date and time for them to check on my work. They just come by and ask me what I am doing and I explained to them that I was starting my sophomore year portfolio. Once I said those words, they were ready to help me in any way possible and willing to give me suggestions.

"All parents seem to feel welcomed into this circle of learning that they share via the portfolio connection."

Even so, Melissa was still pleasantly surprised when:

> My mom accidently [sic] clicked on my freshman portfolio link and she was surprised on how I not only changed physically in a year, but my skills in applying Photoshop and web design.

Chase's mom logged on at 3:20 AM and gave us a glimpse of how the portfolio sharing allowed (or perhaps required) her son to communicate a bit more thoughtfully than the usual adolescent high school male:

> I was surprised and pleased to discover what Chase has done in this class. However, I know that he could have listed a lot more but at this late hour, opted to be "succinct," shall we say. . . . Yes, the online portfolio is a wonderful way for me to see what Chase has learned in your class, since he doesn't often share such information with me—except when he has an exceptionally challenging assignment and wants to vent.

Some of our students come from homes where English is not the language spoken. Students like Bao go the extra mile to share their portfolios. Bao explained to me that he translated his material into Chinese as he shared with his mom. Then, she responded, and Bao translated her Chinese into English to post in our parent forum:

> When Bao had asked me to come look at the computer, I've actually refused a couple of times because I thought that it maybe just another game he may be playing. But after bugging me the entire night, I was actually shown a great deal of excellent work that he put online. I was amazed of how he was able to insert the graphics and pictures onto the computer. When Bao explained the standards to me, I was actually confused, but nodded along pretending I knew what he was talking about. But although I may not understand what he is saying, the program has already proven that they met these standards as I see my child grow as a learner.

Some students dealt with the language barrier by asking older siblings to provide the commentary; two students invited their brothers who were away in college to access the online site, and Fiona's brother responded this way to her work:

> It was really interesting looking at her portfolio. I finally got to know what you all do in this class. It finally gives me proof that she really was asking to use my computer all those times last year for working on Menemac projects and not just for browsing asian avenue or things like that . . . parents and families need to see the portfolios more. I think the idea of portfolios online where the student can't lose them is great enough in itself, but all we need is to be more exposed to it or at least during the process in which they're made.

Whether they be fellow educators or immigrants who speak no English, all parents seem to feel welcomed into this circle of learning that they share via the portfolio connection. Sarah's mom eloquently captures that sense of connection and community that can come from portfolio sharing:

> I enjoyed reading Sarah's portfolio as it helps me get to know that part of her that I very seldom get to observe, her inner thought process. What is amazing to me is how much I can relate to her strengths and challenges; it's almost like reading a page from my journal.

Conclusion

"Part of teaching is helping students learn how to tolerate ambiguity, consider possibilities, and ask questions that are unanswerable."

—*Sara Lawrence Lightfoot*

My underlying goal as a teacher is to nurture in my students the skills and the confidence to be lifelong learners, to foster relationships, and to build learning communities of their own beyond the boundaries of their formal schooling experience. The portfolio has been a powerful tool for my students and me to build for ourselves a strong and supportive learning community, one in which to take risks and "tolerate ambiguities, consider possibilities, and ask questions that are unanswerable."

References

Wiggins G., and McTighe, J. (1998). *Understanding by design.* Alexandria, VA: Association for Supervision and Curriculum Development.

Websites

http://doe.k12.hi.us/
Hawaii Public Schools Website

http://www.ecybermission.com/
eCybermission Program

David Mindorff

David Mindorff, B.A., B.Ed., M.S., has been a middle and high school teacher in international schools in Hungary, Scotland, and Romania and currently teaches high school in Toronto, Ontario. He serves as a deputy chief examiner for the International Baccalaureate (IB) Organization and also serves as biology faculty member for the online curriculum center, a web-based teaching resource for IB teachers. He is co-author of a biology textbook, *IB Diploma Course Companion: Biology*, published by Oxford University Press, 2007.

Assessment Case Studies: IB Theory of Knowledge and Biology
by David Mindorff

School Context

I teach at an independent girls' university preparatory school in Toronto, in the province of Ontario, Canada. It is the rare graduate of our school who does not go on to study at university. Our students are preparing for a dual qualification: i.e., they are working toward an Ontario Secondary School Diploma (OSSD) and also toward a qualification from the International Baccalaureate (IB) Organization.

Our first group of IB students took their exams in May 2004. Initially, our students could elect to pursue an individual IB course certificate or they could aim for the full IB diploma. Currently, all of our students pursue the full IB diploma. The diploma program requires students to follow six courses from each of the traditional disciplines. In addition, students must complete three other requirements: a course titled Theory of Knowledge, an independent research inquiry called the Extended Essay, and a program of experiential learning called CAS (Creativity, Action, and Service).

The IB Organization creates a set of standardized exams that are administered in May of twelfth grade, after two years of preparation. The exams are set and graded outside the school, and results are returned in July. In addition to exams, each course has a program of set course work that differs from subject to subject. The teacher evaluates this work, but the grading is externally moderated to ensure that teachers are not being too harsh or lenient. Each type of course work has defined rubrics that aim at particular skills.

Our province is recovering from a period where entry into domestic universities was highly competitive due to what was termed the "double cohort"—a year when twice as many students as normal were competing for places at university. For this reason, my twelfth-grade students have a preference for constant, clear communication about where they stand in terms of the grade that will be sent to universities.

*"This year we have elected to do away with calculated grades and evaluate using **level descriptors**."*

As an independent school, we are under close scrutiny by the Ministry of Education in terms of our compliance with its directives. We have worked particularly hard at matching our assessment practices with these directives. Ontario teachers are required to assess both formatively and summatively in four categories: knowledge and understanding, thinking, communication, and application.

This year we have elected to do away with calculated grades and evaluate using *level descriptors* (essentially, report card rubrics for course standards). These are written descriptions of what performance would look like for each standard of performance. Student assessments over the grading period are considered as a whole and the best fit description is used to determine the final grade. These level descriptors are based on a synthesis of similar tools used by the IB Organization, in combination with the Ontario Ministry of Education achievement charts. We are convinced by the research, which suggests that comments and feedback provide much more opportunity for learning than calculated grades. Even though final grades based on level descriptors are summative, they communicate more to students and parents about the progress of the learner, and they help the teacher focus his or her instruction on the needs of that particular student.

Figure 1 ▼

Distinguished Achievement

- Demonstrates a comprehensive understanding of the strengths and limitations of the various *Ways of Knowing* and of the methods used in the different *Areas of Knowledge*
- Consistently demonstrates a comprehensive understanding that personal views, judgments, and beliefs may influence their own knowledge claims and those of others
- Demonstrates an exceptional capacity to reason and reflect critically, showing insight
- Consistently identifies values underlying judgment and knowledge claims pertinent to local and global issues
- Consistently demonstrates a balanced approach to inquiry by evaluating claims and counterclaims
- Uses concise and precise oral and written language to formulate and communicate ideas clearly
- Displays exceptionally supportive seminar behaviour including consistently referencing the ideas of others, consistently encouraging the participation of others, and constantly listening and contributing to discussions
- Writing is structured excellently with a logically coherent development leading to an effective conclusion
- Journal exceeds standards for all aspects
- Consistently makes highly effective connections between and across a wide variety of *Ways of Knowing* and *Areas of Knowledge*
- Consistently makes effective connections between personal experience and different *Ways of Knowing* and *Areas of Knowledge* (journal)
- Consistently demonstrates a comprehensive understanding of knowledge at work in the world

The challenge has been to synthesize IB requirements, provincial requirements, and leveled assessment into a coherent assessment process—all the while trying to maintain the trust of twelfth-grade students who might perceive that their high-stakes "grades" are being experimented with.

Classroom Context: Theory of Knowledge

The two classes I teach are twelfth-grade IB Theory of Knowledge/Philosophy and twelfth-grade IB Biology. Theory of Knowledge is a seminar course that is a requirement of the IB diploma. The course requires that students reflect on the strengths and limitations of reason, emotion, language, and perception. Once this is completed, students undertake a critical evaluation of the knowledge claims and methods used in the different disciplines.

There are two summative assessments mandated by the IB. One is a *persuasive essay*, which is a response to a choice of one of ten synoptic questions set by the IB and published at the beginning of each year. The essay is marked by an examiner outside the school. Two recent examples of set questions include:

> Sometimes we hear reasoned arguments that oppose a view to which we are emotionally committed; sometimes we hear a passionate plea for a view we have good reason to reject. Bearing this in mind, discuss the importance of reason and emotion in distinguishing between belief and knowledge.
>
> and
>
> If someone claims that both the division of knowledge into disciplines and the division of the world into countries on a map are artificial, what does this mean? What is the nature of the boundaries between Areas of Knowledge, in your view?

(Citation: © International Baccalaureate Organization, Vade Mecum, 2005)

The second task is an individual or group presentation that requires application of Theory of Knowledge (ToK) content and skills to "Knowledge at Work" (i.e., to apply ToK content to an everyday example). This task is graded by the teacher but contributes to the final IB grade. An example of an effective presentation from this year involved an exhibition of plastinated corpses at the Ontario Science Centre. Two students attended a panel discussion involving the artist who created the exhibit, along with representatives of various ethical perspectives. The students kept detailed notes regarding the claims made by the various participants and centered their presentation around an evaluation of the claims made by the panelists.

As a seminar course, ToK is marked by informality and discussion and the expectation that each individual's unique perspective and experiences will be shared. I have taught ToK for nine years and have always struggled with methods of assessment that will promote behavior that allows students to get the maximum amount out of their seminars. The main reason being that "participation" in traditional grading systems doesn't count for much, and evaluating participation is viewed by students as being highly subjective. Furthermore, according to Ontario Provincial Ministry of Education (MoE) directives, participation would normally be addressed as part of Learning Skills, which do not form part of the final grade. Yet in ToK, if a student doesn't attend to the discussion or doesn't contribute, the quality of the learning goes down considerably. Without participation, the teaching quickly becomes transmissive and students do not develop the know-ledge and viewpoints that will enable them to perform well on the summative tasks.

In our school, classes meet every other day for eighty minutes in the second semester of eleventh grade and the first semester of twelfth grade. As the IB program is new to our school, my class is quite small—there are only eleven students in the class.

"Self-assessment is followed by peer assessment, followed by teacher assessment, and lastly by teacher evaluation."

Example: Assessment of Seminar Performance

At the beginning of the course, students were given the definition of a seminar and the etymology of the word. Together we came up with a list of objectives of a seminar and then proceeded to generate a list of things that would provide evidence of what good seminar behavior might look like (Figure 2a).

We established that excellent performance in a seminar would involve:

> demonstrating a high degree of understanding of the content, consistently referencing the ideas of others, consistently encouraging the participation of others, constantly listening, independently contributing personal perspectives and sharing experiences in discussions.

Together we established what we meant by these outcomes, and a simple descriptive checklist was created. As a general pattern in the class, self-assessment is followed by peer assessment, followed by teacher assessment, and lastly by teacher evaluation.

Figure 2a ▼

At the end of the first semester, students were asked to complete a self-reflection on how they thought they had done against each aspect of the description. The main purpose of this activity was to reinforce expectations and remind them of the content of the description. In the second semester, I had students evaluate each other's participation. This represents slightly higher

Assessment of a Seminar Performance

Standard	Not Yet Met	Met	Exceeded	Evidence
1. Demonstrating a high degree of understanding of content				
2. Consistently encouraging the participation of others				
3. Constantly listening				
4. Independently contributing personal perspectives				
5. Sharing experiences				
6. Consistently referencing the ideas of others				

stakes for the student than self-assessment, as it is a tightly knit group and they are reluctant to be overtly critical of one another, even when reminded that the feedback is supposed to be constructive.

Keeping data while facilitating a discussion is a challenge for me. One strategy I used was having students facilitate the discussion while I kept a record of students' contributions related to the agreed-upon criteria. While some data were gathered when students acted as leaders, the record lacked specifics and tended to pick up information on just a few students. This is due largely to my divided attention—I must regularly jump in to maintain the required depth of discussion.

"I wish I had introduced online discussion earlier in the course to promote greater learning."

Where I have enjoyed recent success is through online discussions using the school's intranet platform called First Class. Each teacher has a class conference where students can access lesson plans, teacher handouts, PowerPoint presentations, and messages posted to the whole class.

The aspects of excellent performance in a seminar still apply to online discussions. I observed that how students do in these online discussions tends to mirror how they do in spoken class discussions. However, written responses provide a portfolio of evidence that can be referred to in one-on-one conversations, and a ready supply of exemplars for assessment. Online entries also allow students from other classes and adults to view the discussions.

Examples of student entries shown in Figure 2b were based on the following assignment:

1. Read Oppenheimer's farewell address to the scientists at Los Alamos. In the speech, Oppenheimer makes several claims about the motivation of scientists and makes a case for motivation being more important than consequences.

2. Choose one claim made by Oppenheimer in the speech. Discuss the extent to which you agree with the claim.

3. Respond to the statements made by two other students by recording the extent to which you agree with the entries of your classmates. Draw in material we have discussed previously.

In seminars, a pattern of discussion often becomes habitual, with certain students remaining silent while others dominate. One student reported that she found that the online discussions made it easier for her voice to be heard. Others reported that they welcomed the opportunity to think carefully before contributing to discussions.

Figure 2b ▼

Online Discussion	
Student Entry	**Teacher Comment**
Jane: With respect to the quote chosen by Doris, isn't it possible for someone to believe that it is good to learn, but not necessarily be a scientist? so couldn't Oppenheimer's claim be applicable to many different areas of knowledge i.e. historians, artists, mathematicians etc. because "it is not possible to be a _____ unless you believe it is good to learn" -- this would apply to any area of knowledge. The quote I have chosen is: "We must understand that whatever our commitments to our own views and ideas, and however confident we are that in the course of time they will tend to prevail, our absolute ... commitment to them, in denial of the views and ideas of other people, cannot be the basis of any kind of agreement." If we were able to remove that bias of our own views and ideas, then there wouldn't be so many disagreements in our world today. Most of us may understand that it is difficult to come to an agreement when you aren't willing to listen/understand the views and opinions of others, but just because we understand that, doesn't mean we always follow that. As a part of human nature, we tend to believe that our statements are correct, which immediately provides the bias to our own opinions. At the same time, like what Doris said in her statement, a scientist's motivation to do something may be driven by greed, which on a positive note can definitely provide progress to one's views and ideas, but a competitive environment also hinders our relationships with one another in a society.	This is one of four entries made by Jane. Here the student is showing an understanding of her chosen quote, linking it to previous class discussions about science as a social institution. From this entry alone she meets standard one. More importantly, in another entry she discusses the dichotomy between motives and consequences and compares it to violent reactions to art. She asks who "owns" responsibility for the violence—the artist or the perpetrator. This dichotomy is one of the main strands through the address, and for this reason, she exceeds standard one. As a musician, she regularly draws parallels between the discussion at hand and aesthetics. This meets the requirements for standard four. In her other entries, she responds to other students' comments and references the ideas of others as she does in the example to the left. For this reason, she meets standards two, three, and six. Standard five is not yet met, but she could achieve this standard in the example to the left by referring to an example that shows recognition of her own biases.

The discussions occurred toward the end of the third quarter of the course. A similar exercise was repeated twice more. The quality of the second discussion showed an improvement over the first, while the third was optional, to allow students who had not contributed adequately to the first two discussions an opportunity to try once more.

Figure 3 shows the overall and specific objectives from the Ontario Provincial Ministry of Education curriculum document relevant to the Theory of Knowledge / Philosophy course, though admittedly, the assessment encourages students to draw in material from all parts of the course. The online discussions have provided me with evidence of achievement in the Ontario ministry assessment categories. The entries proved invaluable in completing the final evaluation for students. I wish I had introduced online discussion earlier in the course to promote greater learning.

Figure 3 ▼

Ontario Provincial Ministry Expectations

Ontario Ministry of Education **overall** expectations addressed by this assessment:

- Demonstrate an understanding of how philosophical questions apply to disciplines such as physics, mathematics, and psychology

Ontario Ministry of Education **specific** expectations addressed by this assessment:

- Formulate and defend their own responses to some of the fundamental questions in the philosophy of science
- Use critical and logical thinking skills to defend their own ideas about ethical issues and to anticipate counter-arguments to their ideas.

Classroom Context: Biology

Figure 4 ▼

All IB diploma students must study a science. They must also study three courses at the higher level (HL) and three courses at the standard level (SL), the difference being the number of hours of study time.

Like all IB courses, students are expected to be introduced to the skills of the discipline. For HL students, this means that sixty hours of experimental work are required over the two years. SL students must do forty hours. HL students meet for an additional eighty-minute period every eight days.

There are two summative assessments mandated for the IB Biology program. One is an exam done in three sittings, set by the IB and marked by an examiner outside the school.

Planning Rubrics

Planning A

	Complete	Partial
Defining the problem or research question	Identifies a focused problem or research question	States the problem or research question, but it is unclear or incomplete
Formulating a hypothesis or research question	Relates the hypothesis or prediction directly to the research question and explains it, quantitatively where appropriate	States the hypothesis or prediction but does not explain it
Selecting variables	Selects the relevant independent and controlled variable(s)	Selects some relevant variables

Planning B

	Complete	Partial
Selecting appropriate apparatus or materials	Selects appropriate apparatus or materials	Selects some appropriate apparatus or materials
Designing a method for the control of variables	Describes a method that allows for the control of the variables	Describes a method that makes some attempt to control the variables
Designing a method for the collection of sufficient relevant data	Design a method that allows for the collection of sufficient relevant data	
	Describes a method that allows for the collection of insufficient relevant data	

The second assessment is based on the sum of the best two grades for eight practical work criteria. The marked practical work is chosen from a portfolio of assessments done over the two years of the program. This portfolio is graded by the teacher and contributes to the final IB grade. As is the case with almost all IB courses, the teacher's grading is moderated externally to ensure that the teacher is not marking too harshly or too leniently.

The eight practical work criteria are planning A, planning B, data collection, data presentation and processing, conclusion and evaluation, manipulative skills, personal skills A, and personal skills B. As examples, planning A and planning B are shown in Figure 4 (page 169).

The eight criteria assume minimum direction from the teacher. The requirement is that exercises will be sufficiently open ended to enable students to make their own decisions about learning, regarding choices such as the questions they want to investigate, the variables they want to control, and the way they want to display and analyze their data. This often requires training in the use of a particular protocol, followed by other opportunities that allow the student to apply the protocol to an experiment of their own design.

"As they review the work of others, they are being exposed to exemplars of varying quality, as well as viewing a diversity of approaches to the task."

Example: Peer Assessment of Lab Planning

Our students tend to be very conscientious and comply to a high standard when clear instructions are provided. They struggle more with the open-ended nature of the IB scientific inquiry model. In my first year at the school, I found the twelfth-grade students resistant to an assessment model that did not allow them to complete the criteria after two or three attempts. The reason for this was that after each practical activity, I was introducing new factors such as more rigorous standards for displaying data, statistical tests, standards for wording hypothesis statements, and methods of representing random and systematic error. From my perspective, I was moving them along a continuum of scientific skills. From their perspective, I was "moving the goal posts" and threatening their university entrance marks, an even greater concern for them.

Assessment *for* Learning

One change I have made to assist students, while still using assessment *for* learning, is to focus on a specific skill in a formative way, providing feedback followed by a summative assessment. For example, I might ask students to construct a plan diagram. I would assess the products formatively, discuss good examples with the class, and then assign a second plan diagram exercise that I would evaluate. This approach is not without its problems—the most significant being the amount of work involved. Also, even with formative assessment, twelfth-grade students focused on university still expect "grades" as a reward for effort.

Another method I have used involves peer assessment without teacher moderation of the feedback. If enough students provide the feedback, then the students can choose what feedback to accept. Furthermore, as they review the work of others, they are being exposed to exemplars of varying quality, as well as viewing a diversity of approaches to the task. If this is done through the school's intranet, an electronic record of the assessment is available for teacher use at any time. Furthermore, multiple classes can read the contents of the discussions and view exemplars from more than just their assessment partners.

The public nature of the process tends to improve the quality of the students' responses and improve compliance with due dates. Furthermore, the tone is collegial rather than adversarial—which is difficult to achieve as a teacher. Lastly, the more feedback the reviewer gives a student, the more positively it is interpreted—the reviewer is putting in significant effort on behalf of the student. In retrospect, I believe that I should have asked the reviewing students to focus on a smaller number of suggestions—perhaps three main ideas. This would encourage more reviewers to point out big-picture problems.

Figure 5 (page 172) shows some examples of feedback given by students in response to a formative lab assignment. Students had been asked to design an experiment that investigated a variable that affects enzyme function. This is an example of a rediscovery lab in that the experiment is a standard one and the variables affecting enzyme function are clearly described in their texts. The purpose of the exercise was to improve the students' compliance with the expectations of the criteria by having them apply them to the work of other students. Also, it was hoped that students would read examples of plans that complied fully. Each lab group member was responsible for commenting on the plan of each member of another lab group, so that each student received feedback from up to three classmates. The summative assessment lab that followed this exercise was much more open ended—and demanding. However, due to the practice and feedback that had taken place earlier, students were prepared.

Figure 5 ▼

Examples of Online Peer Assessments

Student Feedback	Teacher Commentary
Hey Janet… I read your lab… I think you are missing Planning B…? But for planning A, here are some suggestions: • Your research question is great, i just think that you might want to change some of the wording (and check the spelling) • For your hypothesis. You don't have to but it might look nicer to the assessor if you put it in an 'if…then…' statement. Also, you may want to expand on your explanation a little bit. • Everything is great for your variables, you just need to add in what the controlled variables of the experiment are. • Also, for your materials, its nice and crisp if you add in the size of everything like … 125mL burette. Good luck --Kyong	Kyong is conscientious with the level of feedback she is providing. She is also being nonconfrontational in her approach. I would suggest that she is not specific enough when she is suggesting a wording change. Students could ask each other for clarification on their suggestions if they weren't sure.
Hey Kyong, I am assuming this is your work so here are my comments: In the variables section I would put them in a paragraph form vs. the listed statements…just because it flows better. But other than that you have all the info for the variables part. For your method and materials, make sure that you include all the materials that you need in the procedure on the list, I think you were missing tin foil, possibly the tub of water etc. In your method, I just wanted to know how you would know when all the Hydrogen Peroxide was fully reacted? You are doing multiple reactions so I think having some sort of constant, kinda like in Chem where we put 'X' on a piece of paper to show when the reaction happened (when we couldn't see the x anymore). It is a matter of consistency amongst all the reactions that you do. Also I don't remember if I saw it, but if you have it awesome, but you mentioned recording data at equal time intervals…would that be 5 secs? 10 secs? I think a specific amount of time is needed. I think you might want to mention the surroundings (aka Time and Pressure of the room) just as factors that you need to take into consideration as they might affect the reaction. That is all! --Judy	Here Judy is drawing on a shared experience from chemistry class. I would not be aware that Kyong knew the protocol Judy was talking about so this is an unintended benefit of the peer review process. Judy is systematic in reviewing Kyong's work against the criteria.
Hey Renata… • For the various heats it sounds vague… maybe specify or just say heat • Don't know if it matters but you and Gill have the exact same hypothesis • Perhaps instead of catalase production it should be catalase activity which is measured by the amount of oxygen production? *maybe the size of a potato should be constant… typo- Experimental (procedure part) --Doris	Doris' feedback has been done in a hurry, but it is focused and specific. Another thing I have noted is that students will hold each other to a standard of integrity, though they do not always do it in the comment as is done here.
To Kathryn: Looks awesome. Some general tips!' • in the hypothesis…mention that oxygen production basically symbolizes enzyme activity…otherwise the reader may not make the connection and it seems like your research question and hypothesis are about different things. • in materials, be specific about how much of each material you need (e.g. "1 ruler", instead of "ruler") • in procedure, list size of potato pieces • list the time intervals used…not just "regular" • how are you measuring oxygen production? be specific! hope that helps! see you guys in bio --Jenny	If a reader were to read through just these four examples, it is possible to see they are suggesting similar things but they are also suggesting unique things. It is quite easy to read through all of the class comments in a short period of time and it is likely that collectively all issues would be identified.

Conclusion

The examples given in this chapter represent what I believe to be successful outcomes of recent experiments in assessment practice. The changes occurring in my school require this kind of experimentation. I believe the successes stem from the new capacities made possible by the use of communication technology. Through such experiments, I am becoming increasingly convinced of the need to provide students with exemplars of good outcomes and to involve them in the process of teaching each other.

Websites

International Baccalaureate
http://www.ibo.org/

Ontario Ministry of Education
http://www.edu.gov.on.ca/eng/

Stephanie Doane

Stephanie Doane, B.A., M.S.Ed., is an experienced high school educator with a strong background in assessment practice and social studies curriculum development. She is the recipient of the Maine 2003 James Madison Memorial Fellowship for Constitutional Studies and has consulted at the state level in the development of state standards in social studies. Stephanie currently teaches tenth-grade humanities at Casco Bay High School, Maine's first Expeditionary Learning/Outward Bound high school.

Promoting Lifelong Learning: Creative Assessment Practices in Social Studies
by Stephanie Doane

CONTENTS

The time has come to shift our focus from testing to students, and high school teachers can do this in the place where they know their students best—the classroom. By creating classroom assessment systems that promote learning rather than stifle, that allow creativity to flourish rather than wither, teachers can create for their secondary students a learning experience that better reflects the world of today. By involving secondary students in the classroom assessment process, we can counter the negative effects of high-stakes tests and construct learning environments that invite students to actively participate in their own learning, engage in deep thinking, and promote creative problem solving.

How can involving students in the assessment process counter the negative effects of high-stakes testing while supporting the development of future success for all learners? By using assessment in a formative manner, that is *throughout* the learning process rather than just at the *end* of learning, teachers can quickly become informed in regard to student strengths and needs. By actively involving secondary students in this process, students develop an awareness of self that will not only support success in the classroom, but also in the world outside of school. Together, using formative assessment practices, students and teachers can make the assessment process a dynamic one that supports personal growth, risk taking, and self-discovery. This also helps to develop in students the ability to continue learning into, and hopefully throughout, adulthood. In the complex world we live in today, the ability to continue learning beyond the years of formal schooling is imperative for success.

My own journey to create such dynamic learning experiences for my students continues to this day. Early on in my teaching career I realized that assessment, when used in a formative manner, could instruct and facilitate understanding. I developed assessment practices that frequently checked for understanding and gave students the opportunity to act on teacher-provided feedback. I encouraged students to revise work products based on the feedback provided, and I would re-evaluate the work until we were satisfied. After attending several assessment conferences and taking a class specifically on student-involved classroom assessment, I developed and put into practice an assessment system that fully involves and invites students to self-assess, be reflective, and take risks as learners. I realized through my own reflection that what I was creating for my students was a learning environment that was accepting of mistakes. So often our assessment system punishes such risk taking and, in the process, may limit and narrow learning. I realized that if I really wanted my students to grow as learners, I had to create a safe environment, one in which students would be willing to risk attempting more and more challenging tasks. I have been purposefully working to involve students in classroom assessment now for seven years and I know of no better way to support creative and critical learning for *all students*.

"What I was creating for my students was a learning environment that was accepting of mistakes."

Listed below are just a few of the specific ways teachers can involve high school students in the classroom assessment process.

Student Use of Progress Portfolios

At the beginning of each course, give students time to create portfolios in which they organize evidence of their learning, in the form of four-pocket portfolios. These progress portfolios differ from many portfolios used in elementary and middle school—they focus exclusively on the course learning goals. Have students label three pockets with clear learning goals established by the teacher, and label one pocket with a student-set learning goal for the course. The portfolios stay in the classroom and students visit them periodically in order to organize evidence of learning, as well as self-assess progress toward the learning goals. Students select evidence from their ongoing class work that demonstrates progress, growth, or achievement within the learning goal. For example, a learning goal might be to become a more proficient writer, and evidence of progress toward that goal could be a series of improved scores on test essays.

I encourage students to keep examples of past work, even if the work is not their best, because the focus of the progress portfolio is *progress*. The portfolios can also serve as a basis for conversations with the student about their learning. At the end of the course, students use the portfolios filled with evidence of learning to support success on a reflective final exam (explained later) or summary of the course (see below).

Figure 1 ▼

Student-Involved Conferences

A few weeks into each course, I ask students to participate in a conference on their progress using the format set forth in *Conferencing and Reporting* by Gregory, Cameron, and Davies (2011a). Students have prepared for the conference by previously visiting their portfolio and placing in it their early evidence of learning. The conversation should focus on student learning and evidence of that learning (from the portfolio). This gives both the teacher and the student the opportunity to either affirm or adjust the learning goals (from the progress portfolio) based on feedback from those involved in the conference.

Figure 2 ▼

Student: J Subject: US History	Term: 3rd Quarter Date: 3/10/04
Strengths/Accomplishments	**Work samples to show**
- My goal at remembering facts - Group work is well organized and strong participation.	- Two tests to compare my accomplishment and increase in knowledge. - Group project grade and reflection piece
Areas needing improvement	**A goal for next term**
- Using well thought out information and necessary facts in my writing.	- I want to improve on my writing with vasts amount of well thought out information

My closing statement: The most important thing I want you to know is …

- that I enjoy your class and the way you structure the learning. I learn much more in the atmosphere you are teaching in

From Gregory, Cameron, and Davies, *Conferencing and Reporting*, 2001; 2011.

Use of Student-Set Criteria

In most secondary classrooms, teachers establish the criteria that are used to evaluate student work products. Another approach that involves students more directly in owning the criteria is to invite students, with guidance from the teacher, to establish the criteria for major work products (reports, presentations, investigations, demonstrations, exhibitions, and essays). The criteria can then be used to create rubrics, checklists, and other tools for peer and self-assessment while the work is in progress. The same criteria can be used in final teacher evaluations by assigning value (both numeric and descriptive) to the student work based on the criteria. A process for involving students in criteria setting is laid out in *Setting and Using Criteria* by Gregory, Cameron, and Davies (2011b). This technique is especially useful for supporting student success on long-term projects and group work. For example, early in the school year, I help students set criteria for group work using the prompt, *What makes a good group worker?* All group work is then evaluated using these criteria.

Figure 3 ▼

<table>
<tr><td colspan="3" align="center">**Student-Set Group Work Criteria***</td></tr>
<tr><td>**2nd Block US History and the Modern World**</td><td></td><td>**3rd block US History and the Modern World**</td></tr>
<tr>
<td>
1. Participated and had good attendance

2. Did fair share of work and fulfilled responsibilities

3. Picked up the slack when necessary

4. Brought in constructive ideas

5. Is open minded and cooperative with others
</td>
<td></td>
<td>
1. Is dependable, comes prepared and shares responsibility equally

2. Is a collaborative worker, cooperates, participates, and is flexible

3. Makes an effort to contribute, to be creative and innovative

4. Has respect for others, is a good listener, and accepts others' ideas

5. Has a positive attitude
</td>
</tr>
<tr><td colspan="3" align="center">* Students use the criteria to self-assess and give focused feedback to their peers.</td></tr>
</table>

Use of Student Check-Ins on Long-Term Projects

Long-term projects are always stressful, especially when tossed into the busy lives of today's high school students. Whenever students are involved in a project that requires days or weeks to complete, periodically check in with students. Take the time to ask each student (during class) how things are going, what still needs to be done, and what problems they foresee to successful completion of the project. While check-ins do not require that the student necessarily produce evidence, it is a great way for students to assess their own progress. By sharing this information as a class, students have the opportunity to self-assess and learn from their peers. As their teacher, you can get a sense of student progress on the project as well.

Opportunities for Students to Act on Descriptive Feedback

If feedback is going to support student learning, then students need the opportunity to act on that feedback. Build into your course assessment system the understanding that students should and will act on all forms of feedback, including teacher feedback. This can apply to class work, projects, writing assignments, and tests. In many high school classrooms, teachers evaluate work products, hand the product with the evaluative feedback back to the student, and that is it.

But that is not where the learning should end. In fact, feedback becomes much more valuable when students know they have the opportunity to use it as a guide to improve their work product. If corrections or changes are needed, students use the descriptive feedback to make the necessary changes, then submit the product for evaluation. If you wish to promote a learning environment that encourages risk taking, then you should not apply a penalty for initial mistakes. Rather, focus on the progress and learning that has occurred as a result of student effort.

"A reflective final grants students the opportunity to identify patterns of growth."

Opportunities for Students to Be Reflective

At points throughout the course, give students the opportunity to stop and be reflective about learning that has taken place thus far, as well as the learning to come. Consider, as well, the use of a *reflective final* rather than a comprehensive final in the exam format (see Figure 4, page 180). A reflective final gives students the opportunity to self-assess in a comprehensive manner at a crucial time—before they leave your class. A reflective final grants students the opportunity to identify patterns of growth and communicate their learning in an authentic format. It gives you the opportunity to see each student's learning in a format focused on evidence and arranged in such a way that supports the learning goals of the class. Teachers can then use the opportunity to determine a final course grade that is truly reflective of student progress and growth—something that may not always occur if the final course grade is dependent solely on student work products or tests.

Figure 4 ▼

Final Exam: Reflective Summary	**Name**	_____
Doane—US in the Modern World		

Directions:
1. Use your **progress portfolios** as your source of evidence.
2. Follow the directions under each heading.
3. Place evidence, reflections, and evidence for reflections in portfolio and submit as your final exam.

I. DESTINATIONS	II. CONTENT UNITS
• Proficient writer • Productive researcher • Collaborative group worker • Student created	• African-American Experience in the 20th Century • Boom and Bust in 20th Century America • 20th Century American Legal History • America Becomes a World Power • Modern Foreign Policy: Vietnam and Iraq

A. Evidence

1. Find and organize evidence that demonstrates growth, progress or achievement in **each of the four destinations.**

2. Label each accordingly using the sticky notes.

3. Place the evidence in the appropriate pocket.

B. Reflection

1. **Choose one destination** in which you feel you grew or achieved the most.

2. Reflectively write about your growth or achievement in that area addressing the following prompts:

• *Specifically how have you grown or achieved in this area? (Discuss evidence.)*
• *Why is this skill or area important?*
• *How could you use this skill or area in the future?*

3. Find and label **evidence** that supports your assertions.

4. Place the reflection and evidence within the first portfolio.

A. Evidence

1. Find and organize evidence that demonstrates growth, progress or achievement in **four content units.**

2. Label each accordingly using the sticky notes.

3. Place the evidence in the appropriate pocket.

B. Reflection

1. **Choose one content unit** in which you feel you grew or achieved the most.

2. Reflectively write about your growth or achievement in that area addressing the following prompts:

• *Specifically what have you learned about America from studying this unit? (Discuss evidence.)*
• *Why is this information important?*
• *How could you use this information or way of understanding America in the future?*

3. Find and label **evidence** that supports your assertions.

4. Place the reflection and evidence within the second portfolio.

Trying to capture the power of these practices in writing is difficult. Even more difficult is the implementation of these practices, especially in high schools, where so often the focus is on the learning of content to support success on summative assessments rather than creative instruction to support complex thinking. Yet it is imperative that we take positive action to better prepare young adults for the world that awaits them outside of high school.

This is a world that expects results and demands evidence to support the results. By involving secondary students in the classroom assessment process, we are promoting not just creative thinking and learning, but accountability as well. We are supporting accountability in its most *dependable* form—evidence that demonstrates the learning behind any summative numbers or grades.

References

Gregory, K., Cameron, C., and Davies, A. (2011a). *Conferencing and reporting* (2nd ed.). Bloomington, IN: Solution Tree Press.

Gregory K., Cameron C., and Davies A. (2011b). S*etting and using criteria* (2nd ed.). Bloomington, IN: Solution Tree Press.

Biographies

Anne Davies, Ph.D., is a researcher, writer, and educational consultant in the area of classroom assessment. She has also been a teacher, school administrator, and system leader. Author and co-author of more than thirty books and multimedia resources, as well as numerous chapters and articles, she travels internationally, presenting to a wide range of audiences. Anne works with educators at all levels, using quality assessment practices in support of student and adult learning. Her complete CV and information about classroom assessment resources are available at www.annedavies.com. Anne can be reached at *anne@annedavies.com*.

Sandra Herbst is a noted system leader, author, speaker, and consultant with over twenty years of experience. She has worked in both elementary and secondary schools and is a former classroom and specialty teacher, school administrator, program consultant, and assistant superintendent. Sandra has facilitated professional learning in schools, districts, and organizations across North America in the areas of leadership, instruction, assessment, and evaluation. Her school and district experiences deeply connect learners to practical and possible strategies and approaches. She is the co-author of two books on the topic of assessment. Contact her at *sandra@connect2learning.com*.

Kathy Busick, Ph.D., is passionate about listening to and learning from the voices of teachers, students, and families—voices that speak their truth and, in so doing, demand that we take a closer look at our own beliefs, actions, reactions, and assumptions. She is currently working on publishing conversations with Pacific Island educators about the cultures of their home and heart, their experiences of schooling as both learner and teacher, and the challenges of walking successfully in both worlds. Her writing focuses on culture and assessment.